T0158983

HEAVENLY RIPPLES

Ahmed K. Nazir, M.D.

authorHOUSE®

AuthorHouse™
1663 Liberty Drive
Bloomington, IN 47403
www.authorhouse.com
Phone: 1 (800) 839-8640

Published by AuthorHouse 05/17/2018

ISBN: 978-1-5462-4299-4 (sc)
ISBN: 978-1-5462-4297-0 (hc)
ISBN: 978-1-5462-4298-7 (e)

Library of Congress Control Number: 2018906099

Print information available on the last page.

TO,
My soulmate, Dr Shahnaz Nazir, whose tender love and constructive criticism keep me on track like the comet round the sun.

- ❖ The Holy Bible says: God created human after God's Own Image.
- ❖ The Holy Qur'an says: Human is created in the best of form, but then would be reduced to the lowest of the low Except those who believed in God, performed the deeds of righteousness and consistently adhered to the truth, for them there is reward, everlasting.

BOTH statements indicate that basic human nature is, Good.

Contents

MANNERS

❖ During a debate in England's House of Commons, one member of the Parliament shouted at another, "The right honorable gentleman has the manners of a pig". In response to a loud protest by the members of the opposition demanding to take back his words he stated, "I retract my last statement the right honorable gentleman hasn't the manners of a pig". (Reader's Digest, July 2013).

❖ One day, I was all formally dressed up except for my shoes. A patient of mine remarked, "These shoes must be very comfortable.

HAVE and hold: Good Thoughts, Modesty, Simplicity, Moderation, Positive Attitude, and Do Not Infantilize anyone. Easy Said than Done.

MAGICAL MOMENTS

❖ Imagine the Scene:
A magician repeatedly insisting that there was something in the bag and the boy every time confirming the bag being empty, and finally, the magician saying to the boy, "Your hand is in it".

❖ Once, a magician said to his audience, "Let me tell you how I became a magician". He then showed the spectators a good size strip of paper written on which, in a vertical fashion, were the words:

FRESH FISH SOLD HERE TODAY

"This phrase", he stated, "Was a window sign displayed at my father's fish shop. One day, as I was looking at the sign, I got a flash. I said to myself, we are not telling people that fresh fish was sold here yesterday or will be sold tomorrow. Therefore, the word, TODAY, here is understood and the sign would remain just as meaningful without it. Also, this abbreviated sign would less likely leave a hurriedly going passerby with an uneasy feeling of missing the last word."

On saying that he tore off the word TODAY, and now the sign read: FRESH FISH SOLD HERE.

"THEN", the magician continued, "I noticed that the word HERE was equally superfluous because there would be no sense in saying, fresh fish being sold there or at someplace else."

So, he did away with the word HERE, and now the sign said: FRESH FISH SOLD. "Then, I thought the word SOLD was also useless because people come here only with the idea of buying fish", the magician went on. Thus, he eliminated the word SOLD also, and now the sign was reduced to FRESH FISH.

"Then, I speculated", the magician continued, "That we always provide fresh fish supplies as the customers could objectively see the fish being fresh. So what is the idea of our telling them something that they would like to ascertain on their own anyway. Thus, the word FRESH was also gone leaving behind the single word sign: FISH.

He continued, "Then, I took a panoramic view of the shop and of the way things were arranged there. I observed that the overall suggestive setting (main sign of the shop and the model of a big fish so visible from outside) was unmistakably emblematic of its being a fish store and the particular window sign was merely a trite which in my surmise may just as well be totally dispensed with." At that point, he discarded the last remaining word FISH, thus resulting into complete disappearance of the entire sign.

"One day", the magician continued, "My father called me and asked me if I knew anything about the sign that used to be in the window"? I replied that I had destroyed the sign because it was not really necessary". My father angrily said, "what do you mean it was not really necessary, it affects my business. Be it whatever I want the sign back, here and now". My father appeared badly inflamed and I was left with no choice". In a twinkle of eye, simultaneous with his proclamation, "That's how I became a magician", he reproduced before the hushed audience the entire sign saying FRESH FISH SOLD HERE TODAY. What followed soon after, was a spontaneous lavish applause.

COMPANION'S MANUAL

[The following section is written in a light-hearted manner in order to give some insight to improve interpersonal communication skills with our spouses]

CONGRATULATIONS! You just attained the companionship of a very fine and ingeniously designed "device" that possesses the potential range of performing from very rugged tasks to very delicate renderings and a host of other built-in adaptive features including speech. Your companion comes with certain features factory pre-tuned. There are no easy-to-touch knobs for quickly adjusting the level of emotions such as fear, anger, sorrow, joy, contentment etc.

By virtue of prolonged and extremely intricate developmental processes, emergence of some aberrations is to be expected (no two are alike). Intelligence is not infallible even under normal operation and the same holds true for the memory storage and recall systems. So, your companion is to be accepted on "As is" basis. Needless to say, that your own ingenuity and programming skills are vitally crucial.

Art of Initiating: There is no need to be begging, however flattering, a blatant outright instigation or shameless exposure would likely evoke a response of rejection. Art of initiating involves, subtle cues, compliments, suggestive tone or gestures, dainty words, artful instillations leading to world-girdling exploration of each other and caressing of the whole body.

For full enjoyment, it is crucial for the couple to be emotionally in harmony with each other.

To avoid surprises, first check your input data very carefully:

If correct, only then press .... Enter or OK

If found incorrect, press .... Error or Cancel

For optimum performance, make sure your companion is well nourished and adequately relaxed. Expecting perfection from your companion would be like asking that it cast no shadows.

WARNING: As best as possible, keep your companion free of all noxious substances, e.g. ethanol, nicotine, hashish, including bitter talk etc.

CARE & MAINTENANCE:

Basically, your companion is self-running, self-cleaning and self-maintaining but would require your attention and loving care. Some jealousy is a part of normal performance. A good tip to keep up with:

"Love is what we give, Respect what we owe".

TROUBLESHOOTING GUIDE:

Lack of response — Check if your companion is turned ON. If deemed to be slumberous then patience is likely to be the best therapeutic measure. Unexpected Responses — First check your entry data carefully. If it is found to be error-free and fault lies in the processing of the information data then seek professional advice.

Occasionally, emergency medical service may become necessary.

Enjoy the finest art of companionship. Wish the best of skill and good luck.

❖ "He who loves not the loved one's faults does not love truly". (Spanish proverb)
❖ "Friendship often ends in love; but love in friendship, never".

(Save this abecedary for ready reference from time to time)

HAPPY MEDIUM

A good thing may not be liked or recognized by all. Some beauty all admire but some beauty many do not appreciate. There is a noteworthy difference between possessing luxuries and enjoying life. Beauty of the Divine Guidance is that it provides the directions for optimally meeting all the human needs, such as:

- ❖ Physical gratification
- ❖ Environmental comfort
- ❖ Social enjoyment
- ❖ Mental enlightenment
- ❖ Emotional satisfaction
- ❖ Spiritual fulfillment

Disharmony in any one or more of these areas calls for some kind of intervention, e.g. adjustment in diet and/or physical activity; medical and/or surgical treatment; environmental manipulation; elimination of negative factors, etc.

In a cultivated society, everyone would have, privacy, protection, respect, security and freedom. All these have to be provided in accurately balanced manner just as the amount of carbohydrates, fats, proteins, vitamins, minerals and water would be in a diet suggested to a particular individual by an expert dietician.

Moderation means that one must adopt a way of modest living. Being over-occupied in satisfying some needs or desires to the neglect of some other needs or duties and then swinging to the opposite end of the pendulum in order to compensate for one's neglected needs is not healthy, and it should never be considered as a normal course of human life that one has to go through prior to one's coming to the right middle path.

No human-devised system, at individual/collective scale, would be as comprehensively suitable for the whole humankind as the Divine Guidance. To follow this Guidance is, being obedient to Allah (God), and name of this obedience is Islam. Islam teaches being good to self and others. Islam advocates encountering injustice, oppression or terrorism. Islam urges humankind to progress in science and technology while remaining obedient to God. Islam preaches moderation.

Islam, in every sphere of life, presents before humankind the highest standard but evaluates each individual according to his/her ability. Prohibitions in Islam stand as a test for being obedient to God. The idea is to help carve out constructive ways of gratifying all human needs rather than to barricade their gratification.

WIT TO WIT

She was a powerfully built, middle-aged woman of large frame. Since, she was Court-mandated for psychiatric hospitalization I did not need to go through much in terms of admitting her to the hospital. Even so, I could not carry out that simple task smoothly because the lady wouldn't give a straight answer to any question. For example, when asked about her age she said, "I am over twenty-one". Regarding her marital status she stated, "I am single but I have fifteen children". When questioned about having any hallucinations of hearing voices she responded, "I heard what the judge said". History was, that in the Courtroom she had spit at the face of the judge.

To complete my paperwork, I asked her to subtract seven from one hundred. She quickly said, "I can't". I asked her to give it a try. She again said, "I can't". Judging her to be very smart, I posed the same question to her in another way, I said to her, "Supposing you have one hundred dollars and you give me seven dollars then how many dollars would you be left on you".

At a slow pace, she said, "If I have one hundred dollars and I give you seven dollars I will be left with ninety-three dollars but why should I give you seven dollars".?

Interestingly enough, during another one of her hospitalization a few years later, she was examined by Dr. Shahnaz Nazir [my wife] on the female prison ward of the same hospital. At that time, she stated to the doctor, "I have had five husbands and none of them died a natural death". The woman, at the time was facing charges of allegedly murdering her husband and had been referred by the Court for inpatient psychiatric evaluation, and, if necessary, treatment.

It would, of course be unfair, hence un-Islamic, to ignore the plea of being not guilty by reason of insanity, but before it is honored, the possibility of one's trying to manage to go out the side-door, as they say, must be ruled out.

The litmus test is, if a thing is fair, it is Islamic, if unfair, it is un-Islamic.

DON'T LOOK A GIFT HORSE ....

A man of about sixty was admitted to the hospital because of profound depression and no will to live. His thinking, his speech, his body movements were all a textbook picture of psychomotor retardation (slowed down mentally as well as physically).

The medication given to him to elevate his mood had been of no avail. All the psychotherapy fertilizer poured over his mind failed to grow any grain of hope in him.

In the medical conference, it was recommended that he should be given a trial of electroconvulsive therapy (ECT). This was discussed with him and such an arrangement was made for him soon after his written consent to receive this treatment (ECT) was obtained.

The morning he was given his first ECT, on the same afternoon I saw him playing table tennis. He appeared in a good mood and replied very well. I was quite amazed to see that unaccountable change in his condition.

I asked our professor of psychiatry how such a dramatic improvement had come by so quickly. His reply to my laconic and eager reply was, "Dr. Nazir, if somebody gives you a horse, don't count its teeth - take it".

Any measure employed on an empirical basis, may not be considered scientific, nonetheless, it cannot be called irrational either.

DISSOLUTION OF A DELUSION

A misinformed person quickly corrects himself/herself after becoming aware of the factual knowledge. But, a really delusional person retains his/her false belief despite evidence to the contrary.

A delusion is the result of an erratic perception and/or processing, by the brain, of some of the incoming stimuli for which there may be a host of reasons. If the mental impairment gradually subsides, the person becomes more and more realistic and a delusion, related to that person's mental impairment, which he or she was absolutely convinced of and held so sternly before, may clear away, bit by bit, and ultimately may no longer remain tenable to him or her.

An attractive young woman in good physical health was so much out of touch with the reality. that she believed she was "Chinese" and belonged to the "yellow race". She had given to herself some Chinese name also. When asked if she could speak Chinese language, she said, "I was born in America, my parents spoke Chinese". She would not admit an obvious fact that her skin color was black. She was admitted to a closed ward in a psychiatric institution.

After a few weeks of treatment, she had somewhat improved and when asked to describe the color of her skin, she said, "At age thirteen, I was kidnapped by Russians and they painted me black".

One day she suddenly stopped me in the corridor, intently looked at my face and then delicately uttered, "You are all right, I just wanted to make sure that you are the real doctor because there is another one who is a copy of you sometimes walks in here, and the only difference between you and him is, that you have a mole on your face and he doesn't".

One day, I told her that her brother and sister had come to visit her. She said, "I have none", and she refused to see them. On further improvement, she said, "I have no brother but do have a step-sister". After some more improvement, she said, "I have a full sister and a step-brother". After about four months of treatment at the hospital, she had acknowledged her real name, and said, "I am proud to be black". On their last visit to her, she recognized both of them as her full brother and sister, and embraced them passionately. She was discharged from the hospital in the custody of her family with the recommendation to continue her treatment at the community clinic on outpatient basis. She was not cured of her mental illness but she had markedly improved and was no longer delusional.

It is interesting that the delusion of a relatively healthy individual is much less amenable to treatment because it is more likely to fall within the realm of possibility, hence, extremely difficult to be challenged.

True faith (belief in God) is not a delusion. It is not a product of mental illness. There is a divine spark, set in every individual, to help develop the true faith in her or him. Its insistent call, if constantly and consistently ignored by a person, would eventually become inaudible to that person.

PHYSICALLY IN AMERICA BUT ....

History, related by a patient was that while he was leading a troop in a jungle war, suddenly faced an enemy attack and he saw that his buddy was killed in the combat. Quite soon after that, he himself was shot and was moved to a nearby hospital where he was operated upon. On waking up, he was stunned to discover himself lying in the morgue. The moment, they observed his body move the hospital staff right away rushed him to ICU (Intensive Care Unit). Subsequently, he was transferred back to America. A bullet still lodged in his chest was surgically removed but he remained under medical treatment ever after, not for the physical wounds he had sustained but for the resulting mental injuries.

He also gave history of once watching his own body walk by crossing the street right in front of him while he himself, feeling strangely confused, had abruptly halted in the middle of the street.

One day, he said to me, "If I tell you that I can fly, will you believe me"? I said, "No". Then, he said, "If I take you to an open solitary place and fly around you, will you then believe me"? I said, "Yes". Then he said, "But when you come back to the people and tell them what you saw, they will think something is wrong with you, and fearing that, you would be very reluctant to talk about it". After describing this picture to me, he uttered, "That is exactly how I feel about describing some of my experiences to others".

It had taken him twenty-eight years to come out of silence about his personal experience of finding himself lying on a stretcher in the autopsy room.

He would generally prefer to be in a situation of danger or some kind of emergency. He stated that he would rather be at a place where all that would matter would be survival, e.g. in a forest. In that way, his keen sense of duty of being constantly alert would fit well because, under such circumstances, it would be essential for survival. He would always see himself a misfit in the city and stay on guard even when not warranted. Out of no fault of his, he would feel responsible for his buddy's death., and quite often express his feelings of survival guilt.

He was oversensitive to noise. He was highly prone to give a startled response. His waking state was full of flashbacks of war, and his sleep meant war-related nightmares. Physically in America, but in his words, "As far as I am concerned, I am still in Vietnam".

In addition to deriving some benefit from the medication and psychotherapy, he found an airy solace in his firm faith in God. Without the power of his spirituality, he would, perhaps be an inpatient instead of being an outpatient at the VA hospital clinic. Could that be just a placebo effect? I don't think so.

PARADOX

OF the following statements, both are True OR both are False OR if only one of them is True then which one?

    A. Earth is closest to the sun during mid-winter and farthest from the sun during mid-summer.

    B. Diluted nitric acid will corrode steel, while concentrated nitric acid will not.

Some of the truths appear contradictory but are nonetheless true. It isn't until you look a bit deeper that the real grains of wisdom emerge. Both statements cited above are true.

AL-Qur'an **5:** 51 says, "O you who believe! Take not the Jews and the Christians for your friends and protectors to each other, and he, amongst you, that turns to them is of them. Verily, Allah guides not a people unjust".

AL-Qur'an **5:** 5 says, "This day, things good and pure are made lawful unto you. The food of the people of the Book is lawful unto you and yours is lawful unto them. Lawful to you are chaste women who are believers and chaste women among the People of the Book, revealed before your time, when you give them their due dowers, and desire chastity, not lewdness, not secret intrigues. And whosoever rejects Faith, fruitless is his work, and in the Hereafter he will be in the ranks of those who have lost".

Apparently, above-cited Verses are contradictory bur are valid in their own right. Former is applicable at National level in political sense, and latter, at individual level in social sense.

No Qur'anic Verse is abrogated or is superseded by any other Qur'anic Verse.

A REBUTTAL

Someone, with reference to Al-Qur'an: **4:**11, brought up a point that there is a simple mathematical error in the Qur'an thus trying to invalidate the supreme authenticity of the Holy Qur'an. The point raised is:

"The shares in the inheritance, according to the Holy Qur'an, are 2/3rd for the daughters, 1/6th for the mother and the father each and 1/8th for the widow. But, if you add all these you get 1.25 instead of 1, thus not enough inheritance would exist to distribute to all these people".

Response:

Apparently, there does seem a mathematical error in the above-quoted distribution of the inheritance. However, a focused view of this situation would lead us to divide the total asset into 24 units because that is the least common multiple of 3, 6 and 8. Now, the widow would receive 3 units [1/8th] and the parents 4 units each [1/6th]. Thus, 11 units have been distributed. Now, 2/3rd of the remaining 13 units would go to the daughters and 1/3rd of this still left over may go to other relatives or the orphans or the poor.

 ❖ If the sum of the digits of any number regardless of their order is a multiple of nine, that number will also be a multiple of nine.

THE SPIRITUAL BEACON

The Basic Message of all the Divine Holy Books is essentially the same!

The Qur'an is the last Holy Book that continues to be a source of light forever. Holy Qur'an addresses everyone but only those who are seriously interested in it and well-motivated for receiving the guidance will benefit from this Book, and this is the first stage of being a Muttaqi [one who carries due regard for Allah [God} in his/her heart]. Allah has provided this guidance so that we are not left with any pretext. Everyone's actions will be graded on the Day of Judgment. Holy Qur'an is the touchstone according to which every individual's actions are to be tested for them being "sterling" or "counterfeit" in order to be paid back in the same "coin" in the Afterlife.

The Holy Qur'an is a great miracle and is the best gift to the human race. This Book openly invites all people to emulate the distinctive quality of its brilliant text and its eloquent message. Human intellect has always remained paralysed against meeting this challenge effectively. The Holy Qur'an, indeed is a magnificent, graceful and enviable blend of right guidance, cardinal knowledge, effective literary style and charming musical quality that plays on heart's strings. Even today, a considerable number of people all over the world know the Qur'an by heart.

Holy Qur'an, through Divine Revelation was revealed to Prophet Muhammad peace be upon him who taught this Book as directed by Allah, and his very active and vigorous yet integrated life is an exemplary practical demonstration of the Holy Qur'an before us. It is notable that Prophet Muhammad peace be upon him was unschooled.

RIGHTEOUS DEEDS

Deeds of righteousness include but are not limited to:

- ❖ Being kind to your parents, to your relatives, to the orphans and the needy.
- ❖ To speak to people nicely.
- ❖ To pay the Zak'at (distributing 2/12 % of net assets, annually.
- ❖ To establish Sal'at (five times daily Prayer).
- ❖ Fasting as prescribed.
- ❖ Performing Hajj (Makkah Pilgrimage) at least once in one's lifetime if one can afford to.

Performing deeds of righteousness in service of God is, Islam anyone earnestly practicing so is, Muslim.

Righteousness Score (Taqwa Score) = the degree of devoted trust on God + amount of deeds of righteousness minus amount of involvement in evil and sins.

FOOD FOR SOUL

- ❖ Righteous actions
- ❖ Cleanliness
- ❖ Honesty
- ❖ Modesty
- ❖ Patience
- ❖ Music
- ❖ Remembrance of Allah

CONQUEST OF MAKKAH

PROPHET MUHAMMAD PEACE BE UPON HIM had attacked Makkah as a last resort since it had become an inescapable alternative.

Muslims achieved victory and thereafter a big crowd was gathered.

PRESENT there were also who Had:

MADE repeated murderous attacks upon Prophet Muhammad peace be upon him

WOUNDED Prophet Muhammad's pbuh blissful face that also involved breaking of a tooth

SUFFOCATED Prophet Muhammad pbuh by wrapping a piece of cloth around the neck

MURDERED the dear uncle of Prophet Muhammad pbuh, cut off the nose and ears, removed the eyes of the dead body, took out the liver and chewed it

TIED with ropes, Hazrat Bil'al, Hazrat Emmar, Hazrat Saheeb, Hazrat Zaid (may Allah be pleased with all of them) and dragged them on hot stinging sand.

PROPHET MUHAMMAD peace be upon him had a full hand on the enemy. That was the time to take a just revenge. The Muslim soldiers with their swords drawn were ready to behead the enemies of Islam without any delay, they were only waiting for the word.

FEAR-RIDDEN, the defeated were trembling like a leaf. Prophet Muhammad pbuh, at that time, asked them, "Do you have any idea of what I am going to do with you today"? Being stunned, they all amidst a state of hope and despair cried out, "You are kind and the son of a generous father".

INSTANTLY, Prophet Muhammad peace be upon him candidly declared, "Today, there is no penalty on you, you all are free".

NO matching example of such a graceful forgiving exists in the whole history of humankind.

DISTORTIONS

AL-Qur'an **3:** 186 says, "You shall certainly be tried in your possessions, and in yourselves (endowed faculties), and you shall certainly hear much that will grieve you from those who received the Book before you and from those who worship partners besides Allah. But if you persevere patiently and guard against evil, then that indeed is a matter of great resolution".

AL-Qur'an **73:** 10, 11 say, "Moreover, be patient with all the abuse that they who disbelieve shall speak. Thus part from them with a fair parting. AND leave to ME the beliars, those of prosperous ease and bear with them a short while". In other words, "Have patience with what they say, persevere in spite of what they utter, and depart from them with noble dignity. Leave ME with the rejecters, possessors of plenty, and bear with them for a little while".

The Holy Qur'an allows paying one back only in the same coin but gives a higher rank to forgiveness. Now, a party says that the above-cited Verses are no longer valid. They were revealed at the time when Muslims were weak. As soon as Muslims gained power Prophet Muhammad had taken an initiative and murdered those who had uttered blasphemy thus, justifying execution for committing blasphemy. The party claim their carrying extreme love for Prophet Muhammad peace be upon him and claim to have no hesitation in sacrificing their lives for the sake of Prophet Muhammad peace be upon him. This is a glaring example of, in a tricky manner, distorting the history and falsifying the noble, sublime character of Prophet Muhammad Peace Be Upon Him.

what ALLAH, in Al-Qur'an **68:** 4, directly addressing Prophet Muhammad peace be upon him says, "For, Behold thou keepest indeed to a sublime way of life". "Truly you have a strong character".

NOW, the party should be considered as laudable Muslims OR perhaps unconsciously, they themselves are culprits of blasphemy? You Be The Judge!

APOSTASY

Unlike blasphemy, apostasy involves action but still we need not compel anyone to retain a Faith against one's will. An Apostate may revert at some point during his/her lifetime, who knows.

Ai-Qur'an says, "There shall be no compulsion in religion. And whoever of you turns back from his religion, then dies when he is an Unbeliever, these, then their deeds go in vain in this world and in the Hereafter. Whoever believes the Messenger he then surely has obeyed Allah but in case any turn away we have not then sent you as guardian over them. Certainly, there are those who believe then disbelieve, then believe and again disbelieve, then go on adding to Unbelief, Allah will not forgive them nor guide them on the Way. O You who, believe, should anyone among you renounce his religion, soon will Allah bring forth a people whom Allah will live and they will love Allah, they will be humble towards the Believers, mighty against the Rejecters, striving hard in the way of Allah and never afraid of a faultfinder. This is the Grace of Allah that, Allah bestows on whom Allah pleases, and Allah encompasses all and knows all things."

(Ref: Al-Qur'an: **2:** 256, 217; **4:** 80, 137; **5:** 54)

UNBRIDLED LOVE

Greed, Hatred, Impulsivity are not necessarily negative emotions. Like all emotions, it depends on how any particular emotion is handled. For example, greed to acquire knowledge, hatred to stay away from dirty things and impulsivity in performing a righteous act would all be admirable. Jealousy and envy may be used in a good or bad way. You are jealous of what you have and you do not want to leave or lose it at any cost. You are envious of what someone else has and you would very much like to have it. This way, life is a test to see how one manages one's endowed faculties and emotions and how one treats others.

❖ Supposing:
B intensely loves C
D makes some derogatory remark about C
B goes ahead and kills D for insulting C.

Would you admire B for his great love and respect for C?
OR
Condemn B for demonstrating poor control of his/her anger and taking disproportionate revenge?

❖ How much or how little one has control over one's emotions determines one's spiritual strength.

HUMAN RIGHTS

All human beings are not born equal, they all have equal human rights, i.e. fulfillment of their basic human needs such as OF:

Food, Clothing, Shelter.

Freedom of expression.

Freedom to choose Lifestyle, Faith, Career or Life-partner.

Needless to say, those who work for more, do deserve the right to have more, e.g. to possess more wealth, to enjoy greater luxuries of life corresponding to their input.

During a discussion, a party said to the other, "I totally disagree to what you have said but I will fight to the last moment in order to preserve your right to say it".

In an ideal Moral Society, people would be free, to do the things they themselves feel committed to without being hurtful to others.

LOVE

- ❖ Love is perhaps the highest universal human value. It is an intense feeling of deep affection.
- ❖ Love may demand sacrifices.
- ❖ Love is primarily one-sided.
- ❖ Love may beget love but does not demand it.
- ❖ Love accepts, as one is, forever.
- ❖ Love lasts, lust does not.

    Love, must be distinguished from lust-under-the-garb-of-love.

- ❖ "He who loves not the loved one's faults does not love truly".

PATIENCE

Patience involves:
Suppressing of unlawful desires and ignoring every greed and temptation that is not permissible and giving up every gain and pleasure accruing from unlawful ways and means.

Adhering to the bounds set by God, carrying out the duties enjoined by God, and bearing loss and suffering faced on the way of the truth.

Sacrificing one's time, wealth or utilizing one's abilities in good cause, and doing what we should, without grumbling.

Keeping one's emotions, e.g. love, anger, jealousy, joy, sorrow under one's control.

Someone had once said, "I want to be polite to everyone but there do come up some that make it very difficult for me to be so to them". Just as there are different levels of playing a game in order to test our level of skill, similarly, life brings to us different situations that would test our level of patience. Allah expects us to show patience in every situation, e.g. making rational decisions while facing extremely emotional situations.

Tolerating brutality is not patience rather one should try to remedy any such situation.

Self-respect is non-acceptance of cruelty without letting patience leave one.

CONTROVERSY IN UNANIMITY

The topic is paradoxical.

Both, India and Pakistan keep on saying that they want to be on friendly terms with each other but controversy keeps creeping in to prevent it. Kashmir issue between them can easily be resolved by letting Kashmir people to freely decide what they want for themselves.

Everyone wants justice but when justice is done, quite often, it is not accepted.

Unanimity is, that elections should be free, unbiased and conducted peacefully. However in practice, controversy does manage to squeeze itself into the unanimity.

There is unanimity over this that terrorism is a terrible thing but whenever a party takes an action against terrorism controversy comes in because it becomes difficult to distinguish between offenders and defenders.

OF REASON

Humans and animals, both possess passion and intelligence. However reason is the crowning mental or rational attribute of human as distinguished from the intelligence of the animals. We may define reason as that which is thought or alleged as the basis for any opinion, determination or action.

The *Cause* of any event, act or fact is the power that makes it to be. *The Reason* of or for it is the explanation given to it by the human mind.

"He who will not reason is a bigot, he who cannot is a fool, and he who dares not is a slave".

IT would be good to know that:

- ❖ Some conceal truth knowingly
- ❖ Some mix truth with falsehood
- ❖ Some dispute about things of which they have no knowledge

KNOWLEDGE AND WISDOM

Knowledge is information acquired through experience.
Knowledge is the cumulative culture of human race.
Knowledge is a clear and certain apprehension of truth.
Knowledge comprises the information of all fields.
"Knowledge is a process of piling up facts, wisdom lies in their simplification".

Wisdom is the power of true and right discernment, conformity to the course of action dictated by such discernment.
Wisdom, sometimes called common sense, is good practical judgment.
To know that tomato is fruit is knowledge, not to serve it in fruit salad is wisdom.

❖ We need to have the correct knowledge to find the right way of life and the wisdom to use our knowledge in a right way.

WITH PASSAGE OF TIME

Many years ago Dr. Ved P Sharma, now a well-to-do pulmonologist, had stated to me, "Life is difficult". I had differed and said to him, "Life is easy".

On meeting him a few years later, he stated, "Life, if not difficult, is not easy either". Giving a thought to that statement of his a few years later, I said to him, "Life, if not easy, is not as difficult either as some people make it so for themselves".

A few more years had passed by when I had a chance to meet with him again, and then he said, "Even granted that life is not difficult, it certainly is not as easy either as we are trying to make it".

For one to have a goal to be satisfied in life is quite understandable. After all, pursuit of happiness in life is everyone's right.

GOOD AND BAD

Many things, e.g. Internet, television, poetry, atomic energy, our emotions, our faculties etc. can be good or bad depending on their use. "What is potent for good can also be potent for evil".

Competitiveness is good in trying to excel others in performing righteous deeds.

SO, what is good and what is bad?

One idea is, "Nothing is good or bad, it is our thinking that makes it so". According to this idea, we may safely make any choice that would please us or that we may feel like without having to bother to know what might be the right or good course of action in any given situation.

Another idea is, "Good is good and bad is bad". According to this idea, when facing any situation, we would be required to distinguish between good and bad. This would also mean that we ought to do what is right and must not do what is wrong regardless of whether we like it or not.

Then, there is an idea that what God tells us would determine what is good or what is bad, and as such, it is a matter of being obedient to God.

A primary task of life for us is to learn and be able to differentiate between good and bad. Adhering to goodness and continuing the pursuit of truth cannot go unrewarded in the final determination.

We owe it to ourselves to seek correct information and knowledge that would help us to be in concord with Nature and not to be discordant with it. "Whatever befalls in accordance with Nature shall be accounted good" (Cicero - 106-43 B.C.).

Another way would be to see what is beneficial and what is harmful. Some, are interested only in what is effective and what is not.

It is quite amazing that some behavior of the animals we appreciate and some behavior of them we depreciate. The question here is, how come we do so? Obviously, this shows our passing of judgment on the animals according to some standards that we have already set up for us. It is an irrefutable matter that the well-being of humanity lies in deriving the standard of goodness and badness from the holy Qur'an. We need not do anything to prove ourselves being human, that we have already been made by Allah, the thing to be seen is how well do we maintain this ceremonious enthronement entrusted to us. Without being humane. we would become lowest of the low.

CORRUPTION

Corruption includes but is not limited to the Following:

- ❖ To destroy morally.
- ❖ To lower materially the purity of a thing.
- ❖ Illegal ration hoarding.
- ❖ Being guilty of corrupt practices while holding public office.
- ❖ Defending corruption
- ❖ Bribe taking.
- ❖ Bribe giving (Al-Qur'an: **2:** 188).
- ❖ Destroying crops and people's lineage (progeny) **2:** 205

ATTIRE

A husband and a wife are a dress of each other, i.e. they are close to each other, they cover each other, they protect each other.

Covering one's private body parts is perhaps human's instinct, weather and cultural norms serve to extend it. Like their preparation of food, people of different cultures dress themselves differently the basic purpose essentially being the same, i.e. nutrition in case of food, and covering in case of dress. Skin covers and protects the underlying body structures dress covers and protects the skin and protects from the extremes of weather, a protective cover can be decorative though. However, basic function of the dress is to cover, not to reveal the body, and for females, in addition, to protect from lustful eyes. A female's dress sharply defining her curves is not a modest dress for her.

Like one's temperament and manners, one's dress also reflects on one's personality, e.g. one's, conscious or unconscious, show off tendency or attention-seeking intention. Since, the behavior can be unconscious, an immodestly dressed person is not necessarily immodest. One should be appropriately dressed according to the occasion or the situation at the time. Generally, a clean, comfortable, modest and adequate dress should do.

Shame has the same relationship with an individual's dress that his/her personality has with it. Of course, shame and personality do not exist in dress but one's dress does to-a-great-extent reflects one's personality and it can serve as an index for one's level of modesty. A company sells a triangular piece of fabric to effectively cover the cleavage and its immediate surroundings otherwise eye-catching due to wide low-neckline attire, they call it "modesty panel cleavage cover".

❖ An item at a souvenir shop saying: "We do look down upon on low necklines".

❖ A man used to pray," O Lord, Bless me but not in disguise".

ON COMMUNICATION

All living beings communicate. We need to communicate to express our thoughts, feelings, needs and desires, and to teach or to learn. We communicate by our body movements, by our words, by our dress or lack thereof. In other words, we cannot Not communicate.

People are quick in making an opinion about someone and that is very difficult to change afterwards. How we come across to others, first fifteen seconds can make a difference. One's first ten words can tell what respect one has for the other. Hence, first impression can be the last impression.

Nowadays, there are various ways of communication available, However, lack of communication or its misinterpretation is one of the major causes of many problems. Lack of communication functions as a fertile ground for the prejudice to flourish. Needless to say, that it is crucial to make sure that the other party has understood exactly what you mean, and by the same token, to ascertain that you have understood exactly what the other party means to convey.

SHAME AND MODESTY

Shyness is lack of confidence or assertiveness with a tendency to embarrass easily. One is made to change color is an expression used for one who readily blushes.

Shame is not specific to women but relates to men as well, it relates with one's character. Shame, is something colorless, odorless that affects the entire body. It "dissolves" in alcohol. Although, not considering a good thing as good or bad thing as bad is no less than shamelessness but there is little doubt left in someone's being shameless who, despite knowing a thing as being bad, would still continue doing it and would not ashamed of doing it.

Shame is a good thing if it holds one back from doing a bad thing. Natural shame has a charm of its own. The word shame is sometimes synonymous with modesty. Nonetheless, it is a common observation that, as compared to modesty, shamelessness attracts people's attention more readily and therefore it is an easy way to get attention since it comes as a handy tool for attention-seekers. "Modesty is unwillingness to draw attention to your achievements or abilities".

"Modesty is reserve in appearance, manner and speech especially in relation to sexual matters". Since, modesty is still valued and considered admirable in every society one may, consciously or unconsciously, utilize it as an implement to enhance one's charm. While true modesty is highly admirable, false one is contemptible. A person lacking the element of modesty would be like a room devoid of fresh air. An individual, without any trace of modesty in him or her does not deserve the label, "human", in true sense of the word. Modesty is such an important element of humanity that, in its absence, humanity would be at the point of breathing its last.

Modesty is sweet and pleasant. A consistency in politeness, tenderness and good manners is modesty. Modesty brings a method, an order, a grace, elegance, a beauty, a good taste and a good disposition to one's behavior. "Nothing can atone for the lack of modesty".

The perfect personality of Prophet Muhammad peace be upon him, was, from head to foot, a glimmering visage form of modesty.

INDOCTORINATION

During our psychiatry residency program, residents rotate to different supervisor every three months. One day, a supervisor said, "A good thing about this training program is that the residents get a chance to learn good points of every supervisor". At that, professor of psychiatry remarked, "Trouble with the residents is they pick up bad points of every supervisor".

There is no substitute to providing, children education and training at physical, mental and spiritual level and establish in them good habits and moral values, e.g. kindness, patience, honesty, modesty. Setting the rules and the limits and implementing them with consistency and kind firmness are the hallmarks of disciplining.

When I began to take driving lessons the very first thing the Instructor asked me whether I had done any driving before. I said, "Not at all". He said, "That's good. For many of those who have already developed bad habits, we have to work harder to break those habits. In your case, we will not let you develop any bad habit".

CLEANLINESS AND PUNCTUALITY

In the process of developing a good character, ignoring cleanliness and punctuality would be a disastrous start. Interestingly, both of these are also the criteria for being obsessive-compulsive. This shows how one can turn even a virtue into a nuisance or something undesirable. Someone had once said, "My house is clean enough to be hygienic and dirty enough to be comfortable". Cleanliness brings in the element of prevention of dis-ease. It involves, keeping one's body, mind, spirit as well as one's environment, clean.

Punctuality means being on time. Being punctual is one thing knowing the art of being punctual is another. The art of being punctual is to know where you can be on time by being how much late and where you have to be how much early in order to be on time. Lack of punctuality can adversely affect one's business or it may even mean loss of job.

SIMPLICITY

Simplicity, admirable though, also carries negative meanings attached to it, e.g. lack or deficiency of good sense or intelligence.

Simplicity is the state of being simple. It is freedom from admixture, ornament, formality, ostentation, difficulty or subtlety.

Naturalness, Unworldliness, Trustfulness, and beauteous Modesty is majestic Simplicity.

Classic simplicity is not the other name of dullness. Rather, it is one of the things un-ostentatious, everlasting elegance devoid of unnecessary extras.

Simplicity is not easy to model after. Rather, it is one of the things most difficult to imitate, paradoxical it may seem though.

Simplicity is the fashion that would never become old-fashioned.

PROCRASTINATION

Procrastination is an addictive, self-defeating behavior based on lack of self-regulation. It is difficult to effectively, confront a procrastinator because plenty of reasons can be cited to favor or defend it. For Example.

- ❖ It is admirable not to be hasty
- ❖ Getting into something, you are not certain about can be risky
- ❖ Next opportunity can be far better
- ❖ Doing a thing that may not come out to be perfect would not be worth it
- ❖ When facing two difficult choices, wouldn't it be smart to stay aloof, after-all why to take an avoidable responsibility
- ❖ There is no thrill in doing something when there would be plenty of time lying ahead
- ❖ "I perform better under pressure"

Unfortunately, all such justifications do not turn out to be of any benefit to the chronic or habitual procrastinator.

Procrastinator may do away from reality for a while but not forever. A time comes when it would be too late. There is no use crying over spilt milk. On facing, the consequences of his/her own laziness the procrastinator may try to seek refuge in alcohol or other intoxicants. Procrastination can be major cause of one failing or achieving far less than what one could.

ON POLITICS

The word Politics, like many other English words, has its positive as well as negative meanings.

A politician is the one who would practice the principles of civil government, and would intervene in public and private affairs in a reasonable manner and to a reasonable extent. However a politician may also mean as the one who engages in politics for personal or partisan aims rather than for reasons of principle. It may also mean, a political schemer or an opportunist.

A politician is one who can predict what will happen after such a such time, and then would be able to explain, why it didn't.

A friend of his asked a politician, "May I know the secret of your getting elected"?

The politician replied, "All those who knew me voted for my opponent, and all those who knew my opponent voted for me, and it so happened that more people knew him".

- ❖ Election Times: "When air is filled with speeches and vice-versa".
- ❖ "He knows not when to be silent who knows not when to speak".

PSYCHIATRY AND POLITICS

Psychiatry involves every field of life because it relates to human's feelings, thinking and conscious and unconscious deeds. When one joins any party or administration then often one's action becomes in accordance with that party due to which one goes ahead to carry out some such act that is not in accord to one's moral value and one would never do that in one's own personal life. This shows how important it is the duty of the leader of a party.

In the struggle of politics there is an opposition like atmosphere. Each League or Party tries its best to prevail over all other Parties or Movements. Each candidate presents before the people his/her view or goal. Usually, they would promise to strive for preventing crime, establishing peace, promoting prosperity of the people, economic restoration, mitigating poverty, improving the education system, health system and to work for development of the country. However, under the table, they have some of their personal goals, e.g. to get maximum votes and to strengthen the chair after getting, elected and then also to work for further promotion. However, when they see disparity between their personal goals and their announced claims then they have to decide which ones to give precedence. The workers as much they are deficient in sincerity, as more they would gear their contrivances, strategies and tricks toward obtaining their personal goals.

In the area of politics, circumstances change rapidly. Political leaders' rank is short-lived and everyone is in search of increasing one's power or fame. One's endeavor is to expand the circle of one's selection, and one's desire is to become a member of important institutions especially of those committees that determine the distribution of resources and wealth. Beyond that, one also learns the tactics to receive the attention and favors from the individuals in high chairs. However, the "power" gained by such a manner makes one so indebted and bound in gratitude to some of one's political friends or the militia that one's own control, power or will becomes of name' sake only. New opponents keep on coming up conspicuously manifesting their splendor, therefore an ordinary politician, in order to keep his/her position, has to kneel down before his/her opponents, and he/she has to compromise on many things on the basis of timeliness or political consideration.

Country's benefit, public's benefit, and one's own benefit, all these three things are in view of a political leader and one wants to fulfill all of these with sincere heart. However, when these happen to be going in opposite direction then one finds oneself bound and the mental tension has a deep impact on one's nerves. Under this severe psychological stress, one comes to take one's political life as a game. Now, by setting a high goal for self, one gets zealously busy in its pursuit and one's entire happiness, joyfulness depends on the achievement of this target set by one, and for its sake one would, if needed, sacrifice some of the principles.

In politics, the general atmosphere is that of doubts and uncertainty. The central theme is that every government individual is after promoting one's rank and plundering. When, the spell of the government's claims and promises begins to wane, then some other enthusiastic individual with his/her aims steps into the field of politics. Sensing the public's disgust and helplessness, he/she becomes their voice. Now, how to know whether one is a cheater or just a juggler or in reality a reformer and is sicere in eradicating society's restlessness and poor economic condition and has the capability of meeting these obligations.

On the other hand, hopeless public starts imagining that he/she possibly might prove to be their savior. So perceiving the circumstances in his/her favor he/she finds it an easy way to put a blame of incapability or mismanagement on some governmental person or institution and to begin investigative activities. In that way, people become satisfied that now finally they will catch the thieves and the terrorists and bring them to justice.

On the other hand, media foment those allegations, and as the heat escalates it envelops a few other people and administrative institutions. Then the legal investigations proceed in a way to get the results that would serve to get the results that would serve for toward achieving one's political goal. That establishes one's fame and public elects one trusting the one as a sincere worker for the welfare and security of the people and the country.

It is quite possible that, under the extraordinary circumstances, e.g. visualizing some impending grave turmoil, one as being a devotee to serve the country, considering it a sacred task, may set aside the law and may "temporarily" appoint self on the key post "to save the country".

MEDICAL PROFESSION ON POLITICS

The Doctors' opinion on a government's proposed Economic Plan:

The Allergists voted to scratch it.
The Dermatologists advised not to make any rash move.
The Gastroenterologists had sort of a gut feeling about it.
The Neurologists thought the Administration had a lot of nerve.
The Obstetricians felt they were all laboring under a misconception.
The Ophthalmologists considered the idea shortsighted.
The Pathologists yelled, "Over my dead body"!
The Pediatricians said, "Oh, grow up"!
The Psychiatrists thought the whole idea was madness.
The Radiologists could see right through it.
The Surgeons decided to wash their hands off the whole thing.
The Internists thought it was a bitter pill to swallow.
The Plastic Surgeons said, "This puts a whole new face on the matter".
The Podiatrists thought it was a step forward.
The Urologists felt the scheme wouldn't hold water.
The Anesthesiologists thought the whole idea was a gas.
The Cardiologists didn't have the heart to say, No".
In the end, the Proctologists left the decision up to some buttheads at the top.

AN EYE-OPENER

Al-Qur'an: **43:** 54, regarding Pharaoh, says, "He took his people to be light and they obeyed him, for they were indeed a sinful people".

Commentary:

"A tremendous reality has been expressed in this brief sentence. When a person wishes to become autocratic in a country and contrives every plan openly to achieve his object - practices every deception and trick, buys and sells consciences, and persecutes and crushes ruthlessly those who cannot be purchased. He, in fact, shows by his actions, whatever he may say to the contrary, that he takes the people of the country to be light as regards their intellect, morals and manliness, and has formed the impression that he can drive the foolish, unscrupulous and cowardly people wherever he likes. Then, when he has succeeded in his designs and the people become his obedient servants they prove by their conduct and behavior that they are actually what the wicked man had taken them to be, and the main cause of their depravity is that they are basically a "sinful people". They are not in the least concerned as to what is the truth and what is falsehood, what is justice and what is injustice, whether the noble traits of character are truthfulness and honesty or falsehood and dishonesty and meanness. Instead of this, only their personal interests are of real importance to them for the sake of which they remain ever ready to cooperate with every wicked person, to yield to every tyrant, to accept every falsehood and to suppress every protest that is voiced in favor of the truth."

HEREDITY AND ENVIRONMENT

Genes give a person an anatomical structure and physiological functions. These are beyond the individual's control. Genes also give a person the ability and potential to act in a number of ways. What would make a person behave in a certain manner is the product of that person's past training, education, and experiences, and what kind of attitudes that person may have developed as a result of them. One is not only what the society made one to be but also what one made oneself through the experiences offered to one by the society. Comparable life experiences make some people better and some people bitter (the same holds true for a successful and a failed marriage). Two brothers raised under similar circumstances may become two entirely different personalities.

Child-rearing is more of an art than science. It requires knowledge, skill and patience. It would be healthy to leave the child to the child's biological need to eat or drink instead of employing forceful feeding that promotes oppositional behavior in the child. Some parents would tell their child to do something that the child is not capable of performing yet. Later on they keep on reminding the child of his/her previous failure at it and would not let the child try at it again even when the child would have grown enough to perform it successfully. That impedes the child's heading toward acquiring autonomy, secures the child's lack of confidence and engenders resentment, anger and frustration in the child.

Every individual, from infancy to old age, goes through various developmental stages and needs help and special considerations at the time of highly significant changes. Weaning and separation from the mother need to be carried out with Kind Firmness technique. Toilet training the child need not be child-parent battle. A child should be appreciated on his/her accomplishing a milestone. Being harsh with them is likely to be a hindrance to their becoming a mature personality.

The human brain is equipped with excitatory as well as inhibitory centers. We need to facilitate a child's good behavior. If we do not let the child's bad behavior go then the child will learn to abandon it.

Mature people do not try to show off. They are prepared to accept responsibility. They have learnt to think to find out what is true and what is false. They are oriented to like what is good and to dislike what is evil. They have regard for consequences. Such are the people who deserve the privilege to do what they like. On the other hand, those who are selfishly pleasure-minded, indulge in destructive behavior and are disrespectful of consequences need to be disciplined.

GENES AND ACCOUNTABILITY

Genetic characteristics are of various levels of density that correspondingly determine our level of control over them. For example, we have no control on solid characteristics. These determine our physical features, skin color, height, etc. Our instincts, hunger, emotions, etc. fall under the fluid category. We do have control over them to a certain extent. At a still finer level, hold of genes is minimal. These characteristics lead to the development of our attitude, habits or type of behavior. As the hold of genes on the characteristics they impart gets less and less, our control and accountability over those characteristics gets more and more. Since, we are not total slaves of our genes we would be accountable for our actions that we could control.

We cannot justifiably defend our bad inclinations because there is a gene carrying them. Inclination toward alcoholism, violence or homosexuality is not justifiable because they have found some genetic evidence of these characteristics in human. Presence of oncogenes in the DNA shows our vulnerability to develop cancer, not our human right to get it. Prohibitions in Islam stand as a test for being obedient to God.

TEMPERAMENT

Temperament is one's characteristic or usual attitude or mood that determines one's reaction to things. It is a manner of doing a thing independent of the type of action or the reason for it.

Bad temperament (in the absence of mental illness) is a sign of immaturity. A person of bad temperament would have an attitude of selfishness, would be inappropriately impulsive, obnoxious, irritable and oversensitive. His temper easily gets better of him. An individual of bad temperament would be lacking in the qualities that a mature individual would have.

Good temperament is a sign of maturity. A person of good temperament would be an introvert and extrovert in a balanced manner. A mature individual has integrity and an element of regularity in his/her activities, has good attention span, capacity to adapt to new environment and keeps his/her temper.

Good temperament is your asset, do not lose it, in other words, one should be jealous of one's good temperament.

ATTITUDE

"We awaken in others the same Attitude of mind we hold toward them". Attitude of trust, acceptance and optimism is healthful.

Skill develops because of an attitude and its practice leads to excellence. With a firm positive attitude, one can achieve or accomplish what initially may have appeared "impossible".

Attitude laced with arrogance, lust, greed, anger, malice, envy, suspiciousness or pessimism is a negative attitude.

Attitude is a small thing but it makes a big difference, a change of attitude can change one's entire life. People's attitude can change their nation's destination.

❖ While an optimist and a pessimist were debating about the glass being half full or half empty, the opportunist was drinking the juice in it.

APTITUDES

Psychologists have observed THAT:

- ❖ REALISTIC People have athletic or mechanical ability, prefer to work with objects.
- ❖ INVESTIGATIVE People like to observe, learn, investigate, analyze, evaluate, or solve problems.
- ❖ ARTISTIC People have artistic, innovating or intuitional abilities, like to work in unstructured situations, using their imagination or creativity.
- ❖ SOCIAL People like to work with people - to inform, enlighten, help, train, develop, or cure them, or are skilled with words.
- ❖ ENTERPRIsING People like to work with people - influencing, persuading, or performing or leading or managing for organizational goals or for economic gain.
- ❖ CONVENTIONAL People like to work with data, have clerical or numerical ability, carrying out things in detail or following through on other's instructions.

Knowing one's aptitudes can be helpful in choosing a career. By taking a related test or through a vocational program one may find out an occupation that one would be likely to do best at.

ON PREVENTION OF VIOLENCE

Most common major sources of violence in the society are, injustice, greed, jealousy and hatred.

Quite often, immature people cause or provoke violence. Mature people have regard for consequences. Those, who are selfishly pleasure-minded, indulge in destructive behavior and are disrespectful of consequences need disciplining (corrective measures). Of course, child neglect and child abuse are a major problem however being over-solicitous about the child is not in the best interest of the child either. Some children are normally slow in learning a skill. Being harsh with them is likely to be a hindrance to their developing a mature personality.

A child or an adolescent, when restricted from having a freedom should be involved in the process of training to handle that freedom constructively and responsibly instead of keeping the individual deprived of it forever. Children and adolescents become rebellious when over-controlled. At the same time, we should not fulfill their unreasonable demands regardless of their type of approach. Let the child experience a taste of such frustrations. A child has to learn that one cannot have one's own way all the time in life. The child will appreciate this strictness later on. Give the youngsters a clear message, e.g. "NO" instead of "avoid unsafe sex" or "do not drink and drive". To set an example for the children, parents should observe the moral values and standards of goodness and badness as given in the Holy Qur'an in their everyday life. Any unfair dealing with siblings can cause destructive outcomes. Any experience of physical or emotional insult lodged in the unconscious of a person, quite out of context, may suddenly and unexpectedly erupt like a volcano with shockingly disastrous effects.

If, children or adolescents perceive that aggression gets rewarded and cheating and lying flourish in the society, then preaching to them the virtues of patience, honesty and truthfulness is not going to be of any avail and may even appear ridiculous to them. Children are less interested in what is good or what is bad however they quickly find out what is effective and what is not effective, what works and what does not, in terms of getting what they want.

Children who feel ignored by their parents may resort to aggressive behavior in order to receive their attention; children should be taught to adopt acceptable means of getting attention and never to seek attention by behaving destructively. Alcohol and other drugs are definitely linked to occurrences of violence. Illicit drug dealing and smuggling should be watched like a hawk, and severely dealt with.

Attempts should be made at all levels to ensure that no person who might use it hazardously gets access to any dangerous weapon. Watching violence in real life or as shown in the media, e.g. on TV repeatedly over a period of years does affect the impressionable minds. Particularly, when the hero shoots the villain or beats him mercilessly it is liked and appreciated. The children gradually become desensitized to the horrors of violence, moreover, they tend to copy the adults and may act out without much guilt.

"Life for Life" or "Eye for Eye" does not mean that one can take the law in one's own hands, such decisions are to be made by the Courts of Justice. Police should protect the innocent. Criminals should not be let to succeed in hiding themselves behind the thickets of law.

Any person deemed to be a high suicidal or homicidal risk should be carefully evaluated and placed in a supervised structured setting until such situation is resolved. Hot weather may precipitate violence. Noise can also trigger a violent episode. Reduction in noise pollution may serve to lower the level of violence.

Once in a while, there is always an outburst of severe violence, which is no less than an enigma however we do not have to be able to predict with certainty the onset of violence in order to adopt suitable preventive measures to minimize its occurrence. Since, aggression is not an inevitable aspect of human but is a product of aggression-promoting conditions operating within a society, man has the power to reduce his level of aggressiveness. Whether this capability is used wisely or destructively is another matter.

ON BRIBERY

A bribe is any gift or emolument used corruptly to influence a public or official action. The giving, offering or accepting of bribe is, bribery.

Take an example in which a government worker (public servant) would not meet people's legitimate needs that fall in his/her jurisdiction of duties, without being given a gift. This distressing situation demands careful attention. First of all, public should not encourage this type of behavior, and then it would be important to determine if this worker is being underpaid for the job or is greedy. In former case, government should give serious consideration to the matter, and in latter case, the worker deserves to be removed from the job for his/her demonstrated corrupt behavior.

Bribery is an evil practice, and if allowed to become pervasive in the society the situation may become one like termites in the house. Both, government and public have an important role to play in order to stop such activity.

The Holy Qur'an **2:** 188 says, "And eat up not one another's property unjustly (in any illegal way, e.g. stealing, deceiving, etc.) nor give bribery to the rulers (judges before presenting your cases) that you may knowingly eat up a part of the property of others, sinfully.

JUST A THOUGHT

In the course of life, in general, all kind of events or incidents continue happening from moment to moment affecting different people differently. An incident of no significance to one may have an enormous impact on another. Some incidents may affect only a few, whereas, some have a global effect. Although, people have always varied in their possessing of temperaments, sentiments and talents, but human nature has always remained the same. I think that the ongoing tussle in Kashmir, Afghanistan and Middle East is but a reflection of human nature. Needless to say, that fighting against human nature is a mission impossible. All Faiths condemn terrorism and therefore must struggle to eliminate it. Trouble strikes when each party sees the other being a terrorist and thus the matter takes the shape of a difficult-to-break circle.

Bombing the "extremists" or "terrorists" has not proved to be successful in alleviating the existing tension. There would be little sense in telling the terrorists, albeit for the good, that the war-related Verses of The Holy Qur'an have been canceled out by the Verses that preach love, friendship and peace. Rather the need is to teach them to appreciate the Qur'anic Verses in their proper context. Islam is a religion of peace or war depending on the situation being faced. It might be that "suicide bombers' are the people who are oppressed, misguided and/or ignorant, and they should be handled and managed as such. We would be doing much good to them and ourselves too, by trying to understand and meet their legitimate demands and needs and providing them adequate food, clothing, shelter and education.

HOMELAND

Some believe, that behind all this overt aggressive approach to fight terrorism, America has a covert motive of controlling the oil resources, and also to crush Islam. America, however denies waging war against Islam. Discrimination against minorities (not in law but in practice) is nothing new in America, but due to various reasons (right or wrong) since 9/11 it probably became more focused on Muslims. Understandably, some Muslims in America would be afraid of getting targeted or discriminated against simply because of being Muslims. Some Muslims try to defend themselves by saying that the few terrorists so called Muslims are actually the hijackers of Islam, they do not represent the Muslim community at large and should be duly punished. They also keep on explaining to others that Islam is a religion of peace, not violence.

Although, discrimination based on language, race or religion is legally unacceptable, it does have its roots in the minds of many people. An individual belonging to a minority group has to over-achieve or outperform (considerably more than what would be required of one belonging to the majority group) in order to receive a certain recognition or position. Under-representation of a minority group among higher levels may in fact be due to discrimination. Understandably, some Muslims worry about their standing out as Muslims. I wonder, if men and women practicing Islam in its true spirit start hiding their Muslim identity then how Muslims would be able to preserve or establish a positive image of Islam in the eyes of others.

Public opinion is heavily influenced by the leaders and by the media. This serves to create social distance between the groups. Thus, less is known about one another and this lack of communication functions as a fertile ground for the prejudice to flourish. "To the degree one is a stranger, one can be easily perceived as an enemy".

There is every reason for one to be tranquilly and encouragingly confident of being a follower of Islam. I believe that there is no country where one may need to be shamefaced for being a Muslim. It is only the "uneducated" that use region, religion or race as their yardsticks to make an opinion about others. Mature people do not believe in rumors or a "popular view" without verifying it for themselves. Mature people do not judge others by their superficial characteristics. It goes without saying that there is no country wherein a good number of mature people do not exist. Under secularism though, America, to a great extent, runs on Islamic principles. Hence, if discriminated against on ground of color or religion, one has the right to obtain justice in the Courtroom.

A Muslim's "homeland" is independent of his/her place of birth. Geographic boundaries are no barrier to a Muslim. A lamp does not have a rooms of its own but it gives light no matter where it happens to be, similarly, a Muslim's character would or should shine out wherever he/she might be.

- ❖ "Home is the place where, when you have to go there, they have to take you in". (Robert Frost)
- ❖ An advertisement of a Real Estate Agency: "We will get you a house, it is your job to make it home".

PONDER AND DO

- ❖ We have bigger homes but smaller families
- ❖ More conveniences but less time
- ❖ We have more degrees but less sense
- ❖ More knowledge but less judgment
- ❖ More experts but more problems
- ❖ More medicines but less healthiness
- ❖ We have been all the way to the moon and back, but have trouble crossing the street to meet the neighbor
- ❖ We produce more copies than ever, but have less communication
- ❖ We have become long on quantity but short on quality
- ❖ Tall man but short character
- ❖ These are fast times of fast foods, but slow digestion
- ❖ Steep profits but shallow relationships
- ❖ It is a time where there is much in the window, but nothing in the room

(Dalai Lama)

- ❖ A Sign at a Church, "What on earth you are doing for Heaven's sake".

"DO IT ANYWAY"

❖ "People are often unreasonable, illogical and self-centered, Forgive them anyway.
❖ If you are kind people may accuse you of selfish, ulterior motives, Be kind anyway.
❖ If you are honest and frank, people may cheat you, Be honest and frank anyway.
❖ You see, in the final analysis it is between you and God, it was never between you and them anyway."

(Taken from the poem by Mother Teresa)

QUR'ANIC LIFESTYLE

The Qur'anic etiquette and lifestyle is the way to make the best of Both Worlds:

- ❖ Worship none but Allah (God)
- ❖ Do not cover the Truth with falsehood nor conceal the Truth when you know
- ❖ Do not speak ill of others behind their back
- ❖ Avoid vain talk
- ❖ Observe faithfully your trusts and covenants
- ❖ Do not walk on earth with an air of insolence
- ❖ Be moderate in your pace and lower your voice
- ❖ Lower your gaze and guard your modesty except with those joined to you in marriage
- ❖ Women should draw their veils over their bosoms and not display their beauty except to their husbands and close members of the family
- ❖ Do not commit murder, stealing, adultery, lying, bribery or indulge in gambling and intoxicants
- ❖ Do not laugh at others it may be that they are better than you
- ❖ Do not defame or be sarcastic to others
- ❖ Do not be pryingly inquisitive. Let not your curiosity trespass the limits of decency
- ❖ Fight for a good cause, e.g. justice and peace
- ❖ Avert evil with good

❖ Make your utterance straightforward. Do not say with your lips that is not in your heart

❖ Give measure and weight with full justice that is better and fairer in the final determination

❖ If, someone (even an impious) comes to you with any news, ascertain the truth lest you harm people unwittingly

❖ Restrain anger and pardon people

❖ Do not envy those whom Allah has given more

❖ On receiving a courteous greeting, meet it with a greeting still more courteous or at least of equal courtesy

❖ Do not hold secret councils among yourselves for inequity or hostility and disobedience to Allah's Guidance

❖ Do not sit with them who hold the Message of Allah in defiance or ridicule unless they turn to a different theme

❖ Leave alone those who take their religion to be a mere play and amusement, and are deceived by the life of this world

❖ Eat and drink but waste not by excess

❖ Do not love to see scandal circulate

❖ Pursue not of which you have no knowledge

❖ Humble yourselves in prayers

❖ Make room in the assemblies, and when asked to rise up, rise up

❖ Enter not the house other than your own until you have asked permission and saluted those in them, and if asked to go back, go back. It is no fault on your part to enter houses not used for living that serve some other use for you

❖ If two parties among the Believers fall into a fight, you make peace between them, but if one of them transgresses beyond bounds against the other then fight against the one that transgresses until it complies with the command of Allah

❖ Everything is not fair in love or war. If you have done an act of indecency or wronged your souls, remember Allah and ask for forgiveness, and never be obstinate in persisting knowingly in the wrong you have done. Allah accepts the repentance of those who do evil in ignorance and repent soon afterwards

❖ Be steadfast in Prayer and pay Zak'at (financial due)

❖ Travel through the earth and see, what was the end of those who rejected Truth

❖ Invite all to the Way of your Lord with wisdom and beautiful preaching, and argue with them in ways that are best

PROPHET MUHAMMAD (peace be upon him) has practically demonstrated the Qur'anic Lifestyle, and we all should strive to imitate it to the best of our ability.

GOOD GOVERNANCE

Good Governance is Islamic governance that ORDAINS:

Ensure religious tolerance.

Make a policy that is based on equity. Make sure that general public is happy even at the risk of displeasure of a few big people.

Keep in view, that the army and the common men who pay taxes are two important classes, but in a well faring State their well-being cannot be guaranteed without proper functioning and preservation of the other classes, the judges and magistrates, the secretaries of the State and the officers of various departments who collect various revenues, maintain law and order as well as observe peace and amity among the diverse classes of the society. They also guard the rights and privileges of the citizens and look to the performance of various duties by individuals and classes. Prosperity of the whole setup depends upon the traders and industrialists. They act as a medium between consumers and suppliers. They collect the requirements of the society and exert to provide goods. Make sure there is no black-marketing. Then, comes the class of the poor and the disabled. It is absolutely necessary that they should be looked after, helped and provided, at least the minimum necessities for their well-being and contented living. Keep in touch with the people. Poverty is the actual cause of devastation and ruination of a country and the main cause of poverty of the people is the desire of its ruler and officers to amass wealth, and possessions whether by fair or foul means. The rich always want more.

Ensure an honest judiciary, You must select people of excellent character and high caliber with meritorious records. When they realize that they have committed a mistake in judgment they should not insist on it by trying to justify it. They should not be corrupt, covetous or greedy. They should not be satisfied with ordinary enquiry or scrutiny of a case but must attach the greatest importance to reasoning, arguments and proofs. They should not get tired of lengthy discussions and arguments. They must exhibit patience and perseverance, and when truth is revealed to them they must pass their judgments. These appointments must be made without showing any kind of favoritism or accepting any influence, otherwise tyranny, corruption and misrule will reign. Let the judiciary to be above every kind of executive pressure or influence, above fear or favor, intrigue or corruption.

If your enemy invites you to a peace treaty, never refuse to accept such an offer, but even after such treaties, be very careful. At the same time, be very careful never to break your promise with your enemy.

Do not reserve for yourself anything which is a common property of all and in which others have equal rights. Do not close your eyes from glaring malpractice of officers, miscarriage of justice and misuse of rights because you will be held responsible for the wrong thus done to others. In the near future, your wrong practices and mal-administration will be exposed and you will be held responsible and punished for the wrong done to the helpless and oppressed people.

AMBIGUITY AND VAGUENESS

What is precise may not be accurate. What is ambiguous may not be vague. If a word has two definite well accepted meanings there is nothing vague about it however if its use is in a situation where both of its meanings might be applicable, ambiguity is said to be present and it would be necessary, in the very beginning, to make clear the meaning in which the word is being used.

A term would be vague if defined and understood in different ways and there is no universally accepted definition of it, e.g. "educated", "morality", "obscenity", etc.

"ZARABA"

The Arabic word, "Zaraba" has multiple meanings and it has been used in its different meanings in the Holy Qur'an at places. Interestingly, in Al-Qur'an: **4: 34**, this word is applicable in most all of its meanings., although it has been generally taken in its limited sense and is translated as "beat" the wives. The Holy Qur'an does not advocate domestic violence and gives equal rights to men and women over one another, men have a degree superiority because they support women. AL-Qur'an: **9: 71** says, "Men and women are protectors of one another".

The Verse **4: 34** offers a few options to resolve a grossly disruptive marital situation where the wife would have become outrightly defiant and unmanageable. One option is to bring in two arbiters, one from each side, who would be helpful in resolving the situation, "zaraba".

"Zaraba" means, to admonish, to set an example or to give advice, however If a mutual discussion between the couple fails, one slap (zaraba) can bring about a dramatic change in one's attitude and that may resolve the situation.

"Zaraba" means - to withdraw. Bed separation for a certain time may serve the purpose.

"Zaraba" means - to travel. It may be that the wife likes to travel or to settle at some place else, and the solution may lie in traveling.

"Zaraba" means - to go to earn livelihood. It is quite possible that the wife would be willing to do a job and the husband being against it or the other way round. Going her/his to go to work would resolve the situation.

"Zaraba" means - to express a desire for physical intimacy. Solution to the problem may very well be lying in doing so.

"Zaraba" means - to separate. If nothing works, considering the option of separation with mutual agreement may settle the issue.

❖ A disjointed segmental view of the Holy Qur'an is likely to furnish reflections pretty much similar to the repercussions of the seven blind men taking stock of an elephant in a zoo. If certain Qur'anic excerpts are taken out of context of the specific situation or isolated from the particular circumstances that they are applicable to, then not to say of the people of other denominations, our own confidence in Islam may start getting affected. That for God's sake, what kind of religious is this that apparently accepts inequality between men and women, gives the green light to beat the spouse, allows cutting off of a hand, excites to fight and make war, preaches hatred against non-Muslims, and falls in with killing of people. This subject, I have dealt with in my other books, e.g., "Islam and Obstacles to It".

ETIQUETTE OF DEBATING

An argument is a process of reasoning to establish or refute a position by the use of evidence or demonstration. In any given situation, before plunging into debate it would be important that first a definition of all the keywords in the topic under discussion is established. That would eliminate ambiguity and at least markedly reduce vagueness.

In order to debate effectively, it would be necessary TO:

❖ Stay on the topic under discussion, and try not to drift away from it
❖ Observe patience
❖ Put forward reasonable arguments in a calm manner
❖ Have reliable support to back up the claims. Quoting an authority is not necessarily a valid argument or evidence
❖ Point out problems with the current situation and convince the other party that the problems are significant
❖ Point out the benefits of the proposed change
❖ Avoid emotional reasons or appeal to emotions
❖ Try to understand well your opponent's point of view
❖ Never make personal remarks or insult your opponent
❖ Be a partner, rather than an adversary to your opponent. Purpose should be to learn and arrive at the truth, not to win the debate or defeat your opponent
❖ Not start arguing on a thing that you possess little knowledge of or on any issue that would be of little practical significance

It may be helpful to keep in mind that, "Truth often suffers more by the heat of its defenders than from the arguments of its opponents".

❖ A Parliamentarian said to his opponent, "I totally disagree to what you have said but I'll fight to the last moment in order to preserve your right to say it".

HUMAN AND HUMANE

A human being is one of the human race. Human denotes to what pertains to humankind with no suggestion as to its being good or evil. God has endowed human with all the positive qualities, physical as well as mental, corresponding to the functions which he/she would need to perform. Since the existence of human being, basic human nature has been essentially the same, has never changed.

Humane denotes what we may rightly expect from humankind. A humane person's enterprise or endeavor carries the intention to prevent or relieve suffering. The humane person will not needlessly inflict pain upon the meanest thing that lives. The merciful person is disposed to withhold or mitigate the suffering even of the guilty. The compassionate person sympathizes with and desires to relieve actual suffering while one who is humane would forestall and prevent the suffering that he/she sees to be possible. Kindness, Compassion, Mercy and Patience are the main ingredients of humaneness.

Human, if not humane, would be inhuman (worse than animals). Cruelty, brutality, mercilessness or stony-heartedness is inhumanity.

LAW & ORDER

Law and Order are supposed to, reasonably control, people's beliefs and their desires.

Lawmakers should keep in mind that the Law would serve to create and maintain order and peace in the society and safeguard the welfare of the public, e.g. mandatory vaccination or traffic laws. Standard should set as to establish justice, not to justify public emotions or political demands. Judges should have the freedom to call a spade, a spade, and their safety should be ensured.

It is valueless having fair laws if they are not fairly implemented or fair decisions are not valued. What the boss does may not be what the law states.

The system that suggests cutting the hand off for the crime of theft is justice-based. The system demands first to establish a community in which there would be no poverty, no unjust disparity between the rich and the non-rich. Then, therein, there must be a law that would be sufficient of a deterrent to hold back anyone from committing theft. Stealing theerin would amount to disturbing and upsetting of the established peaceful balance in the community, hence the prescribed punishment.

Those, not morally bound, need to be so legally.

MORAL LAWS

Solids, liquids, gases, waves, rays, etc. have their own specific laws. Moral laws of Nature are just as fixed and relentless as are the other laws of Nature, what one sows, so one shall have to reap. Our built-in Conscience is the seat, foundation or source of Natural (Universal) Human Values.

AL-Qur'an: **96:** 15, 16 says, "If he denies and turns away WE will drag him by the "Naseyah", a lying, sinful "Naseyah". Interestingly, the word "Naseyah" in the Arabic Text of this profound statement has been translated at three different levels of human understanding of these Verses. At physical level, it has been translated as "forelock". Its translation at symbolic level is "forehead" (as it represents individual's part of respect). Its translation at mental (anatomic-physiologic) level is "forebrain" (prefrontal lobe). Prefrontal area of the frontal lobe of the brain located right behind the forehead is responsible for motivating, planning and initiating good or sinful behavior (Note: lying, sinful Naseyah in the above statement) holding the individual responsible for telling of lies or speaking truth, as such.

Natural (Universal) Human Values are based on Nature's Moral Laws. They include but are not limited to the Following:

Honesty, Modesty, Sincerity, Integrity, Speaking truth.

Being fair to self and others.

Being unselfishly helpful to others.

Being kind and respectful to others, unconditional acceptance of others Except, of their harmful habits or behavior.

Abiding by universal human values involves carrying out, the righteous deeds and suppression of unlawful desires. Adherence to the Natural Human Values as a rule and effectively taking to task the violators, would end poverty and terrorism. This is the only way to establish justice in a society, goal here is, to bring about peace and prosperity, not equality.

HONESTY

Honesty is the general character of being honest, i.e. being fair and candid in dealing with others, true, just, upright, trustworthy, chaste, virtuous, free from fraud, equitable, creditable, fair, sincere or frank.

Honesty is a natural human value and is an integral part of conscience.

I have come to understand honesty better by learning its antonyms, e.g. deceitful, disingenuous, faithless, false, fraudulent, hypocritical, lying, mendacious, perfidious, traitorous, treacherous, unfaithful, unscrupulous or untrue.

A person showing any one of the quoted above would be dishonest.

RISE OF NATIONS

Countries, wherein people in a vast majority, would possess, integrity, a sense of responsibility, observe punctuality, would be honest in their dealings, would be willing to work diligently and be productive, would show respect to others and for Rules and Regulations, would be smart enough to prudently save and make sound investments, do become rich and prosperous.

People there would be busy in improving themselves rather than craving to straighten out everyone else's affairs. They would be talking less and working more.

Level of the rise of a nation depends on to what degree that nation observes, Reality Principle and adheres to the universal moral values (natural human values).

FALL OF NATIONS

Countries, wherein public gets divided into multiple Parties or Groups and they would start spreading hatred among one another. On top of that, if injustice prevails, e.g. selections are not made on merit basis there would naturally flourish an element of negative envy and jealousy. People there, would begin to letdown those who would have taken undue advantage over them.

In the presence of corruption and in the absence of just decisions or lack of respect for such decisions, people would become revengeful, and violence would emerge. Any country wherein, such a state of affairs prevails would remain or become poor, would be at the mercy of others, become vulnerable to exploitation by the rich and powerful countries and very likely eventually disintegrate.

Level of the fall of a nation depends on to what degree that nation observes, Pleasure Principle and ignores the universal moral values (natural human values).

IDEAL NATION

Obviously, due to several factors, e.g. color, country, etc., multiple nations have come about, nonetheless, primarily the entire humanity is one nation. As such, an ideal nation would be the one that has a universal message, is justice-based and welcomes all people of all races and all countries to join it, but would not force its doctrine on anyone.

This can only be possible if it invites all people to accept the Sovereignty of One Almighty God, the Creator and the Sustainer of All while ensuring that it would not jeopardize their safety, merit-based opportunities and other basic human rights because of their declination to accept the outright invitation.

Nation, that would practice such a system would be an ideal nation. It would not be confined to any territorial boundaries. Majority/minority concept would not exist in an ideal nation. An ideal nation inviting all with equal opportunity to join it exists throughout the world, sporadically though. Only the individuals make a nation moral, progressive and magnificent.

❖ "If men be good, government cannot be bad".
   (William Penn)

ECONOMY RELATED TALK

ISLAM gives the right of better living to the hard working who exercise their talents constructively. Islam is against extravagance or any undue hoarding of material things. Islam encourages wealth circulation and its distribution, not on equally basis, but in such a wholesome and just manner that it would kick out all undue disparity between the rich and the poor and also prevent its relapse. Islam has due regard for the rights and privileges of everyone, including the disabled or handicapped.

Islam is not against taking a loan when really necessary. A usury system points toward living beyond one's means. Once trapped in it, it becomes extremely difficult to get out of the entanglements of usury, because merciless usury-devouring capitalists have no regard for people unless they can extract usury juice out of them. It would not be inapt to label them as human leeches. They worship money, and have no interest in God. Since the usury system has become bread and butter for the big moneylenders, they make so much propaganda in support of it that even those being ground in its mill tend to believe that this is the only system that is practical in the modern world, and the worst they can think of it is, a necessary evil. In other words, they think that the usury system has become indispensable, and the Islamic Economic System is no longer tenable in modern life. This indeed, is a very pessimistic and defeatist attitude toward Islam. It is a fatal mistake to get blinded by the superficial shine of the usury system.

While usury is condemned in Islam, trading is permitted and enormously encouraged. A legitimate trade or industry promotes prosperity and stability of people and nations, whereas usury ruins the individuals and the countries. In Islam, Zak'at is an obligation (2/12 % of the net assets, annually). In addition, regarding Charity, the Holy Qur'an says, "Give away to the deserving whatever you possess over and above your needs" (AL-Qur'an: **2:** 219).

The following have been suggested to stop the worldwide economic crisis"

- ❖ Learn to stay within your means, at individual as well as at national level, and be content with what you can easily afford. Let not the bigger houses, bigger cars and the worldly splendor get you involved into the system of debt.
- ❖ Refrain from interest/usury.
- ❖ Countries of greater power should not encroach upon the natural resources of other countries. The resources should be used only for the benefit of the very country that the resources belong to.
- ❖ Leaders of nation should be sincere and loyal to their country.
- ❖ Rights of the poor must be recognized and the obligations of the rich to the poor should be fulfilled.

GOLD OR MERE GLITTER

There is a saying that only a jeweller can recognize a real diamond. Yet, even those who lack this ability wish to possess a real diamond instead of a fake one because they know very well that it does make a difference. Obviously, it is important to distinguish between right and wrong, good and bad, and real gold and mere glitter.

A middle-aged lady who died of cancer would never failed to mention this to me on any of her visits. Every time, she would say, "You just take a painting from some famous art museum and remove it from its frame (she would emphasize and re-emphasize that the painting must not be in the frame) and then, have that unframed painting mixed into a pile of several other paintings in the art section of some common department store. Now, if someone leisurely looking at that collection of paintings particularly picks out the one from the museum then that person has the ability to recognize great art." I feel that in a quite innocent manner she had conveyed something very profound.

Allah has kept many things secret from the human being, e.g. what is the realness of the universe, what is soul, etc. but along with it has also imbued the elements of beneficial curiosity and systematic search in the composition of the human being, riding on the hobbyhorse of which the human being is observed traversing the milestones of success in various fields of knowledge, and bringing about so wonderful inventions. With proper software installed, an ordinary box will become a radio or TV whereas the most expensive jewelry box without it will never be.

DEVIL'S TACTICS

Just as honey may be employed to serve as an alluring bait, likewise the *appeal of knowledge* may be utilized by the devil as a delightful decoy to loosen one's grip on Allah's "Trail Rope". Satan's methodology to get the humans under the net is imparting glamour to sin and minimizing its consequences.

Those, whose trust on Allah is firm and possess self-reliance will never fall a prey to the Satan. Some, question and ridicule a person who changes due to a good reason BUT if that person has some refined goal in view and is regardful of the consequences of his/her actions then he/she would be steadfast and observe patience. That is Self-Reliance.

- ❖ "Humanity's values have declined with time
- ❖ Our thoughts are now at odds with the divine
- ❖ Yet those who see the light may still be spared
- ❖ All souls long to be saved and enter Heaven"
  (from a song rendered at Shen Yun Performing Arts)

BASICS

For variety's sake or out of necessity, we may like some novel way of turning the electricity on or off, we may use the sockets of different shapes or sizes, we may safely choose to utilize a different voltage or even a different type of electricity but if we disregard the fundamental principles of electricity then the outcome, at best, would likely to be that the appliance would not run.

Just as we cannot afford to dismiss the fundamental laws of electricity, similarly the basic principles of Islam (God's Guidance) are indispensable. Through non-adherence to this fundamental core any system would be a total flop, whereas any system under any name would be successful by by adhering to this fundamental core. The more closely a system operates on God's Guidance the more organized it is going to be. To see this correlation more clearly take any two such countries where, in everyday life, Islamic "rules of the road" are being practised more in one than in the other. Then, evaluate which country is relatively more disciplined, more stable and more peaceful.

Honesty, Modesty, Kindness, Generosity are universally accepted as basic natural, moral human values. These are the values that make a human, humane.

SOCIAL SKILLS

Greeting others cheerfully, introducing oneself, initiating conversation and being able to maintain it are part of social skills. In general, treat others, as you would like them to treat you.

Possession of social skills means, having the art of treating others to their liking. It involves:

- ❖ Being self-confident
- ❖ Feeling at ease in company without causing discomfort of any kind in others.
- ❖ Being helpful

Not dating does not necessarily mean lack of social skills or timidity it may be due to one's innate shyness or modesty.

Possession of social skills is like having a weapon or a tool in one's hands that one may use positively or negatively. One may employ one's social skills to be helpful to people or to cheat or exploit them just as well. By social skills, one can improve one's business or assert oneself in different situations, e.g. defend oneself against a negative remark, etc. Generally, it would be best to ignore a sexual overture but occasionally, depending on the situation, it may become necessary to short-circuit it, i.e. to pull off one's high horse or to take the wings out of one's sails.

- ❖ One day, I was all formally dressed except for my shoes, a patient of mine remarked, "These shoes must be very comfortable".

ON SEPARATION OF CHURCH AND STATE

One may very well say, Why is it that American Democratic System so widely applying the principles of Islam is not an Islamic System?

The soul-sufficing answer to this touching question is that the basic Islamic principles, although observed in America, are not given the recognition as being from Almighty God (Allah). This means that Allah's Supremacy, in life as a whole, is not duly acknowledged. In this way, the door is left open to usher in such human-devised laws into the system as may even be counter to the Islamic laws, for example, usury, gambling, tobacco, wine, etc. Hence, in order to keep the conscience clear in the resulting messy state of affairs, it is considered necessary to segregate the Church from the State, a fatal dichotomy indeed.

An odious slice in the life of America's president, Bill Clinton (a highly responsible person, is a glaring example of this deplorable earthly dichotomy. Bill Clinton's confession that he had done a wrong thing and at the same time saying, "But I did not do anything illegal", brings up a point to ponder on how can something be legal but not right or something be wrong but not illegal? One cannot help here but to wonder who has determined what is right and what is wrong, and who has decided what is legal and what is illegal?

When Bill Clinton said that he had "broken soul" but "strong heart". It carried the implication that the Church should forgive him and the State let him continue to run the country. It needs to be realized that Church and State dichotomy is just as artificial as mind and body dichotomy.

SCIENTIFIC APPROACH

When civilization was at its lowest ebb in Arabia, the law of the jungle was the rule. Right was not might but might was right. There were lords and slaves, and the slaves were subjected to torment. Women were downgraded, and many newborn daughters buried alive.

But, when those people started to act according to the Holy Qur'an, the whole situation was radically altered. Justice, Peace and Prosperity prevailed in the society. Women received their deserved status, class superiority disappeared and the slavery system was legally abolished.

But then, as much people removed themselves from the Qur'anic Guidance, a proportionate decline in their civilization status emerged. Nefarious elements began to tarnish and fractionate the stately solid structure of the society, and again, once an enviable situation turned into a deplorable one.

Now, the cry of the time, which we must get attuned to, is to re-institute the Qur'anic principles properly, both in our individual lives and in society as a whole. We, as Muslims, should strive to restore the peaceful harmony among people and their environment that existed during the times when the Holy Qur'an was devotedly practised. The approach is scientific, and the task is not insurmountable either.

TWO APART

(A & B)

A

The universe has happened to come into existence as a result of random and automatic physical and chemical processes. And, over an indefinite period of time, it has become transformed into its present form. The work of science is to explain how it all occurred, and how it may progress.

B

The universe has been caused to come into existence as a result of organized and planned physical and chemical processes, over an indefinite period of time, it has been transformed into its present form. The work of science is to understand how it all was brought about and how it is being conducted.

The difference between the above two statements is subtle but significant. The former **A** is a mechanical approach, and carries a connotation that there is no Intelligent Being behind the scene, whereas, the latter **B** is a teleological approach and suggests that some Supreme Intelligence has created everything and is running the show. It is quite easy to understand that the world of the apologist of the **A** school of thought would be way different than the world of the student of the **B** school of thought, even though, both are seen as breathing in the same one atmosphere.

EVOLUTION OR CREATION

One thought is. that if everything has to happen according to physical and chemical laws then what need is there to bring in a creator? However I think that someone would still be needed to prepare a meal despite the fact that the whole process involved for the meal to get ready to eat essentially takes place under physical and chemical laws.

No doubt, through an evolutionary process, over a long period of time, there have come about astonishing changes of color, size and shape in all creations, including human beings, but these changes have taken place within their own limited sphere and genetic potential.

It is noteworthy that only human babies, at birth, need their umbilical cords to be tied (clamped) and then intersected. Even for their survival, human babies remain helplessly dependent over a period of several years. These findings do not fit well into the concept of survival of the fittest as understood in the theory of evolution. These observations indicate that human babies could have not survived had they evolved from the animals. This shows that the human being has been specially created as a unique separate entity and distinct from all animals (Al-Qur'an: **23:** 14).

Having a concept of Allah does not automatically develop ideas of morality. One may develop ideas of morality through self-disciplining, through the teachings of one's parents and/or teachers or by virtue of the Law of the land. Nevertheless, the simple fact is that there has to be present, in the first place, a potential for the development of moral sense. It may be worthwhile to ponder, where did this potential (capacity) to develop ideas of morality originally come from? A fortuitous permutation or purposefully installed? A toy would not walk or talk or perform any function no matter how much battery power is supplied to it unless that particular feature has been built into it. The most expensive jewelry box will not become a radio without the required technology installed in it.

TAKEN FOR GRANTED

Several years ago, I placed an order for a watch. It arrived, as advertised, immersed in a bottle of water. The watch being lifeless was lying still in the bottle, albeit "running". As I brought the wet watch out of the water, I observed that it was keeping the correct time. My amazement was momentary but that timepiece remained a conversation piece for me for a long time. I would enjoy talking with my friends about the unique packaging in which the watch was delivered.

I am pretty sure that if this mode of watch delivery is made a routine procedure it would soon become a thing taken for granted, like a spouse after marriage, and we would not pay due attention to it. I remember once while on a guided tour, a time came when we were casting no more than a casual glance even at those that were supposed to be great works of art. At that, a lady had remarked, "This happens when we have too much of a good thing".

❖ Certain things are such that their presence is not felt but there absence is keenly felt. Ask the one having an attack of asthma, the importance of air.

CURTAIN OF FAMILIARITY

Perhaps, we are hidden from ourselves behind the "curtain of familiarity". We seldom wonder at the splendid "packaging" in which we ourselves are delivered into this world. Imagine a double-layered silken bag of water, strategically anchored in a gift box with velvety lining and a smooth shiny outer surface which in turn is encased, securely hooked, in another shock-resistant magic box. So to speak, we are gift-wrapped, respectably. In scientific terms, we are, from within, enclosed in 1. A membranous wall, 2. the uterine wall and 3. The abdominal wall, respectively. The Holy Qur'an, the Book of Wisdom says that Allah has created you in the wombs of your mothers, in stages one after another, in three veils of darkness.

Our sustenance, in the form of breast-milk, is assured even before our arrival. We arrive in this world quite loudly announcing our accession armed with the weapon of the "omnipotence of helplessness". Our delivery indeed is a *breathtaking* event. Allah, the Highest, in a variety of ways, has invited our attention to so many things, including the phenomenon of our own birth.

GLOBAL VILLAGE

Diversity simply manifests the Beauty of Unity.

A basic belief presented by Allah for all human beings is to acknowledge that prayer must be to One Allah only. Allah has created the universes without a model, has set a proportion of all things and has directed all of creation. All creation is programmed and has no choice except human who has been given the faculty of Reason and then, Freedom to choose whether or not to follow the Straight Path.

What might be a common gathering point for all people on the sphere of the earth that would be suitable to all races of all times.? For this, Allah has designated a place where Adam and Eve, looking and longing for each other, had found each other since them being sent on earth from the Heaven.

Keeping in view the intricacies of human life, it is very easy to see that any system of government devised by human beings, aside from Allah's designated way would not be adequate for all. Classification of moral values as Eastern and Western is far from being satisfactory. It serves little else than widening the gulf between the people of the two hemispheres of the world. Islam means obedience to Allah. Thus, under the umbrella of Allah's Unity, an Islamic way of life can be be promulgated. The Holy Qur'an has the message for the whole world. It would create a sense of international uniformity if the high human values presented in the Holy

Qur'an are put under one rubric term, "Islamic" instead of ascribing them to many different classes.

Allah commands, "Do not reduce anyone's assets, give full measure when ye measure, and weigh with a balance straight, that is better and fairer in the final determination". By adhering to these rules, violence in the world would be observed declining dramatically. Hoping for peace to thrive in the absence of justice would be like wishing to keep live fish without water.

Similarly, for the uniformity of nomenclature, non-observance of the Qur'anic principles would be better called as being "un-Islamic" (disobedience to Allah) rather than be given multiple titles, e.g. un-American, un-English, un-Pakistani, unIndian, etc. etc.

Islam is in concurrence of the Decalogue (Ten Commandments). Islam is against bribery, black-marketing, backbiting, and looking for faults in others. Breach of confidentiality is not something admirable. Directions are given in the Holy Qur'an regarding respect for privacy of others. Thus, by adopting the Islamic principles, a scene of mutual trust emerges.

Allah, in Al-Qur'an: **2:** 62 says, "Verily, those who believe in Prophet Muhammad or who are Jews or Christians or Sabiens (others), anywho believe in Allah and the Last Day and do the righteous deeds, shall have their reward with their Lord. On them shall be no fear nor shall they grieve".

This makes it clear that mere biological belongings to any particular family, group, race or nation is not the determining factor in obtaining an allotment In Jannat (Heaven). A feeling of paying respect to the human dignity of each individual should be in the hearts of all members of the community, government and public.

MODERATE DRINKING

There must be some charm in alcohol that makes people psyched or disposed to it. It is interesting that some "Wines and Liquor" stores carry the sign, "Wines and Spirits". Alcohol is a toxic chemical substance, not a food. It has no place in Medicine for the treatment of anxiety or depression, rather it is a cause of depression. Alcohol, by first depressing the highest controlling centers of the brain, initially makes the person "bold" and shameless. One may commit things under the influence of alcohol that one would be ashamed of doing while being sober. The individual, under the influence of alcohol loses sound judgment. The role of alcohol in causing traffic accidents, domestic violence, etc. is undeniable. Moderation is for good things, e.g. food, exercise, etc. bad things should be avoided altogether.

The Qur'anic Verse: **4:** 43 neither prohibits nor permits anything. Here, the topic relates to certain conditions in which one should not offer Sal'at Prayer - being unclean due to any reason, e.g. after a bowel movement, after cohabiting or being in a state of intoxication (altered consciousness) until one has taken a shower, has become clean and sober and able to understand what one would be reciting. Deriving from this that the Holy Qur'an prohibits getting intoxicated but allows moderate drinking is another example of interpreting the Qur'an according to one's own desire. The Verses related to the topic are **2:** 219 and **5:** 91, 92. Here, the message clearly states that, "Great sin, inherent in intoxicants and gambling far outweighs their benefit. These are abominations and products of Satan's handiwork whose plan is to sew enmity and hatred between people and make them forgetful of Allah".

Of course, The Holy Qur'an gives the human the freedom of making a choice to follow Allah or Satan but not without having to face its consequences. Alcohol and gambling are related to each other in terms of both being addictive, the former causes physical addiction, the latter psychological.

MARRIAGEABLE AGE

Menarche is a sign of puberty, not of marriageable age. On the other hand, a woman may have reached marriageable age and not started menstruating yet. Thus, presence or absence of menstruation is not a criterion to establish marriageable age, it is a guide for the iddat interval (waiting period for the woman before getting married after divorce).

Al-Qur'an: **4:** 6 says, "Trail and test the orphan girls until they are capable of marriage. If you notice that they understand, then hand over their wealth to them".

Fixing one figure for all might not be fair. Having attained marriageable age means that the individual meets all of the following Criteria:

- ❖ Is perfectly competent to make an informed consent and to decide in his or her best interest
- ❖ Understands the nature of the marital contract and is capable of fulfilling the responsibilities entailed in the marital relationship, e.g. interpersonal communication, raising children, his/her own education, etc.
- ❖ Has fully developed physically to safely undergo the situations that are a part of marital life and has also acquired sufficient emotional maturity to constructively, handle the situations commonly encountered after the marriage

Sexual activity before the age of 18 is associated with relatively higher incidence of developing cervical cancer. For the sake of our children's protection, we need to educate them so that, they would not be swayed by peer pressure. To prematurely plunge them, on our own, into those very things that they need to abstain from is indeed amazing, and certainly not warrantable. One is more likely to go through medical/psychological complications and problems related to early marriage.

Basic principle is, if it is unfair, it is un-islamic. Jeopardizing one's physical and/or mental health in any way is unfair, hence, un-Islamic.

❖ "You are forbidden to inherit women against their will" (Al-Qur'an: **4: ** 19).

SEX EDUCATION AT SCHOOL

Basic human rights are the ones a newborn has without any discrimination due to one's gender, language, race or religion. Other rights that one is entitled to receive would be on merit basis. Right to freedom depends upon to the extent one would use it safely and without being hurtful to others.

Unlike, love and poetry, music and sex can be taught. Sex is a strong instinctual drive that if unduly suppressed would find an outlet, one way or the other. It would be unnatural to protect a child from getting involved in sex by keeping the child in dark or giving out to the child misleading knowledge about sex. A child, boy or girl, should be provided correct information regarding sex just as much as the child would be able to handle it constructively before he/she might do something undesirable or get into any kind of trouble because of having little or wrong knowledge about sex.

Parents should provide some basic information about sex to their children but certain details a teacher can explain better. Some parents are against sex education in school because they are concerned their children (particularly daughters) may involve themselves in premarital sex. What they need to realize is, that providing sex education is one thing, teaching moral values is another.

Not socializing at all is not practical. The art of living is to mingle with people, treating them justly and kindly without compromising your own values. One's appearance, movement and attitude toward sex can have an aversive or stimulating effect on another one's sexual desire. Being ignorant of or blind to such an obvious reality would very likely turn this normal activity sour later in one's marital life.

Sex education should just as well include, knowing the psychology of the opposite sex. Lacking the art of keeping the spouse attracted to you can be disastrous. Failure to meet the husband's or the wife's legitimate sexual needs can pollute the clean atmosphere of any marriage. Under the given situation, a point may come where the wife may be left to ponder, what magic the other woman has that she does not know of or the husband may start wondering, what magic the other man has that he doesn't.

SAFE SEX

Sexual liberation has proven itself a "psychological disaster". It has not given the adolescents the satisfaction they have been looking for. Hence, they start seeking pleasure in sexual perversions or drugs or join some cult. Promiscuity is associated with severe emotional conflicts among college students seeking psychiatric help.

One hypothesis is that enjoying total freedom of sex and achieving the highest socioeconomic status are not compatible with each other, in other words, these two things are mutually exclusive.

Despite sex education and use of contraceptives, sexual freedom has brought in more venereal disease (STD), more teenage pregnancies and more empty relationships. Safe sex is getting married and staying faithful.

DATING

The best way to avoid marital problems is, do not get married. The safest way to avoid the problems of socialization would be, not to socialize at all but it is not practical.

It is necessary to make sure that one has developed a reasonable expertise, ability and confidence to effectively, handle the situations encountered in any given field before letting one get into it, and dating is no exception to it. Of course, it would be a mistake to let anyone drive or even cross a street if one would not be able to do so safely. There is no excuse for not knowing the ins and outs or do's and don'ts of a situation and then getting involved in it.

Role of parents is to teach their children and to give them advice with firm kindness, not to impose their will on them. Raising their children was their foremost obligation not to bring it later to remind them of the tremendous sacrifices they had made for them. One's honor or dishonor is not one's family's honor or dishonor. Every individual is responsible essentially for his/her own actions. Not letting anyone to choose one's life-partner is unfair, there is no bar to offering good advice, though. Some keep on looking endlessly for a person who would be an ideal husband or wife for them.

❖ Observed on the packets of a brand of dates: "A date to remember".

SELECTING A LIFE PARTNER

The process of selecting a life partner is quite complex. Even an appropriate matching of the physical characteristics and the level of education of the partners does not guarantee a happy marriage. In general, everyone likes to see a good character and gentle manners in one's mate. Many spend ages in looking for a combination of beauty and riches. Individual idiosyncrasy plays an immense part in this selection process. For a certain man, his would-be-wife should not be very attractive although he may not express it openly what he is really looking for himself. A certain woman may turn down an excellent proposal for marriage because she would feel the suitor being too good for her.

People seek marriage for different reasons. For example (in descending order):

- ❖ Dependency needs
- ❖ Loneliness (for companionship)
- ❖ Sexual desires (mostly men, only 1% women)
- ❖ Unhappy home life with parents
- ❖ Social pressure

Marriage requires putting trust on and being fair to each other. At least, one of them (usually man) should be able to and willing to take the responsibility of providing for the basic human needs of the other on an ongoing basis. Caring, sharing with mutual respect and regard for the partner's likes and dislikes and needs is the hallmark of a satisfactory marital relationship. A third one may horn in between the two but cannot be successful unless there would be some weakness in the bond between the two.

ARRANGED MARRIAGE

In the exclusively arranged marriage system, parents or family members choose a mate for the boy or the girl. Disliking or liking by the girl or the boy of the match made by them is of secondary importance in this system and is quite often completely ignored by the parents. Boy and girl are expected to go along with the decision made for them by their elders regardless of whether they like it or not. They have no say in that matter. If they are unhappy about it they have to swallow the bitter pill anyway.

The big plus of this way of arranging the marriage is that the selection made by the parents is based on their experience in life. A match made in good consideration of the facts, by the mature people, is very likely to prove to be a good thing in future. Many arranged marriages have proved to be very stable and happy. Love develops between the couple through living together after their marriage and it does not fade away with the passage of time.

The negative thing of the arranged marriage system is, that sometimes the family happens to decide on a very unreasonable and grossly unsuitable match for the girl or the boy and then tries to coercively thrust it on her or him. Making anyone to marry against one's will is not Islamic. Occasionally, it may even be that the proposed couple might have never met or seen each other before. A blind marriage may be compared to a high-risk gamble.

NON-ARRANGED MARRIAGE

The advantage of a non-arranged marriage is that the matching is of the couple's own mutual choice. After all, it is they who have to spend their lives with each other. Moreover, they do not want any kind of interference from others in their lives, anyway. Since, it is their own choice they cannot blame anybody else for making that decision for them and, in case of any difficulty, they would more likely be trying harder to stay together rather than to be blaming or cursing those who otherwise would have been the cause of putting them into that relationship.

The disadvantage of this approach "love marriage" is, that sometimes the young folks, based on their immaturity, go by their emotions and happen to make unrealistic commitments and very often wind up in a very unsuitable relationship. They, unlike purely, scientific-minded, may have wild romantic orientation and would fervently plunge into ventures, Probably, they do not realize the importance and seriousness of the responsibilities and of the values tied to the commitment. They pay no heed to the advice of their elders and they lose contact with their families. Sometimes, their family members feel, insulted, and would not hesitate to resort to extreme measures against the couple even if the match in itself might be very becoming and reasonable.

Some parents prefer meeting of the boy and the girl first and to come into the scene only after they have expressed their liking for each other, whereas, some parents would like to see the boy or the girl first before introducing them to each other.

By keeping the Islamic approach in view, all those concerned in the matter would display open-mindedness and would be willing to accept and greet a reasonable and suitable match for marriage no matter from which side it might be coming from.

REGARDING IN-LAWS

In-Laws add another dimension to the life of a couple. Mature people take it as an addition of a variety (spice) in their life. They would meet the new relatives in a neutral manner, with clean slate. They would directly communicate with one another and try to learn about one another with the idea of developing an understanding relationship. It is a challenge but generally they make it, fruitfully.

On the contrary, some would often get carried away by their preconceived negative orientation about in-laws, and as such, they would have a tendency to interpret even the most innocent interaction or situation in a way that would serve to create a distance between them rather than to bring them closer. A recently married friend of mine had once said, "Same events occur but, after marriage, their interpretation changes".

Whether a husband should take the side of his wife or his mother OR whether a wife should go by her husband or by what her parents tell her to? These are difficult, controversial and trying questions, indeed.

One answer given to this question was that, after marriage, legally the spouse becomes the nearest relative and one should feel obligated to take the side of the spouse, as such.

The other response to this question was that respect for the parents should receive priority since this relationship is biologically based, one can have another wife but mother is only one.

Regarding the given issue, if we keep ourselves limited to the above two arguments we will continue to stay in conflict, forever. However, if we ask the same question by adding, "always", to it, e.g. whether a husband should always take the side of his wife or always the side of his mother, it would probably make one think more seriously into it. Since, each situation can be different and challenging, a better approach to the question would be, "It depends on the individual situation". That would automatically lead one to methodically investigate the matter at hand every time like a disinterested person, and then arrive at a just decision without being disrespectful to any party.

Money issues exert a significant impact on marital relationship. For example, how much to spend on dresses and cosmetics and parties. Sometimes, one partner may want to provide financial help to his or her family members but the other one does not like it. Regarding this matter, the couple would need to put their heads together in order to arrive at a decision of mutual agreement that would be realistic.

In most cases, professional help would not be required, but the possibility of seeking Family Therapy should be considered for any situation that the family members cannot prudently resolve within themselves.

❖ Just as it may come out after a long time how bad a certain person is, it may also take one a long time to come to realize how good a certain person is, in both cases, previously not seen thus.

PSYCHOLOGICAL CONFLICT

Whenever one comes to face a situation calling for a difficult decision to be made in favor of one thing or the other it creates, in one's mind, a psychological conflict, e.g. to be or not to be OR to bed/wed or not to. If we could love a thing 100% or hate it 100% there would be no problem. It becomes a problem when the heart is tearing between two objects. Psychological conflict is a state of mental anguish that destroys one's peace of mind.

Many an immigrants do develop a psychological conflict in terms of deciding which country to permanently settle in. A victim of domestic violence usually feels conflicted in seeking a way out worrying lest asking help might get her/him into more trouble. A rape victim is afraid and feels ashamed of expressing out her feelings. A husband may have to think whether to go by his mother's choice or abide by his wife, and the same situation the wife may encounter. The problem further intensifies in case it becomes a matter of ego or there would develop a situation of power struggle.

Some feel divided between fulfilling their religious obligations and conducting their worldly affairs, For them, these two are separate things and are mutually exclusive. Islam prevents development of this dichotomy. If, one would have complete faith in the Day of Judgment, would abstain from things prohibited in Islam, would continue to offer one's religious rituals along with adequately taking care of one's worldly affairs then, the world and the religion, for the one, would cease to be two different things.

Thus, one would be, without conflict, successfully traversing the Straight Path, and at the same time, fulfilling both obligations. For, a religious individual there is nothing that does not fall in the realm of religion. For such a person religion is not limited to the performance of a few rituals it is a way of his/her everyday life.

ANGER

Anger is a violent vindictive passion. It is a strong displeasure due to injury (physical or mental), mistreatment or opposition. It is personal and usually selfish. As a rule, it is easier to feel than to think. It is easier for one to act out one's emotions than to go by reason. It is easier to express anger than fear.

Anger, like love, may be reasonable, unreasonable or without any reason (reason not known). Some keep their anger suppressed at surface level and maintain an air of superficial friendliness (pseudo-mutuality), such a state of affairs is not healthy. Inviting the other party to politely discuss and resolve the things may serve, not only to establish an understanding of a higher grade between them but it will also quell the pinching mental irritation persisting due to the unexpressed anger. Unresolved anger may burst anytime and cause preventable disaster.

Taking a few deep breaths, drinking some juice or cold water, retreating by one stage of comfort, e.g. sitting if standing, some positive thinking, exercising control or leaving the site, are all helpful in dispelling the anger.

- ❖ "If you are right there is no need to be angry, and if you are wrong then you do not have any right to be angry".
- ❖ Good Temper, is your asset do not lose it.

ISLAM gives top credit to overcoming one's anger and forgiving. (AL-Qur'an: **3:** 134)

FEAR

Fear is an emotion excited by threatening evil or impending pain accompanied by a desire to avoid or escape. One who is timid would be more liable to become fearful. People develop specific fears as a result of learning. The brain structure associated with fear is amygdala. Fear may be in the form of reverence where it is a feeling of profound respect mingled with awe and affection. If one is dependent on or love someone, one would be afraid of disobeying or displeasing the figure, e.g. fear of God. one may be afraid of one's wife.

Many people are ashamed of expressing their fear. They would rather become angry or may prefer to suffer in silence. Fear and/or anxiety are dominant factors affecting life of most all human beings, differently though. The difference between fear and anxiety is that the former is realistic and rational and the latter, unrealistic and irrational.

Fear can be a manipulating and controlling factor in an individual's life. Appeal to fear is a tactic by which a person attempts to create support for an idea by using deception and propaganda in attempts to increase fear and prejudice toward competitor. The appeal to fear is common in marketing and politics. Fear, uncertainty and doubt can create a situation in which buyers are encouraged to purchase by brand, regardless of the relative technical merits. Fear is an effective tool to change attitudes.

STRESS FACTORS

What is stressful for one may not be so for another. However, certain things that are well established to be stressful enough to have an adverse effect on physical or emotional health of most all include but are not limited to the Following:

- ❖ Domestic problems
- ❖ Breakup of a close relationship
- ❖ Financial difficulties
- ❖ Stingy boss
- ❖ Traffic hassles
- ❖ Hustle and bustle of city life
- ❖ Polluted air
- ❖ Noise pollution

In terms of causing an elevation of one's blood pressure, noise has its impact regardless of whether one feels bothered by it or not.

Some other things that can have a significant psychological impact on one's health are: onset of puberty, aging, marriage, divorce, loss of job, sickness, death of a close relative or a friend, moving, a constant fear of possibility of meeting some loss or encountering some kind of tragedy.

People may react to their real or imagined circumstances in a variety of ways, For Example:

❖ Some, instead of facing a challenging situation, turn themselves away from it and fall into a false sense of security.

❖ Some have so much to say, but are either themselves unable to talk about their feelings or they are threatened, lest they open their lips.

❖ Some of them may protect themselves by developing a state of "psychic numbness" or "emotional anesthesia", they show diminished responsiveness to the external world, as such.

❖ Some, with a heavy heart, accept their life situation in silent despair.

❖ Some, in search of peace of mind, vainly indulge themselves in deriving pleasure from a variety of material things.

❖ Some submerge themselves in alcohol or other substances. They feel great, that in this way they can control their moods, but they do not realize that by such doing of theirs, they are only transiently feeling better, not getting better.

❖ Some, consciously or unconsciously, start hurting others physically and/or emotionally by letting out (displacing) their frustrations or anger on them.

COPING WITH STRESS

Society is the system of community life, in which individuals, ordinarily in a territorial establishment, form a continuous and regulatory association of their mutual benefit and protection. In order to cope with everyday life, we must all have some understanding of social structure, our position in it, its rules and regulations, divisions and hierarchies, and the way that other people will interpret situations in which we are involved.

In general, some useful armaments necessary for effectively and constructively coping with the stress of life situations ARE:

* Good physical and mental health, required for the maintenance of which are, cleanliness, adequate balanced diet and comfortable sleep
* Self-confidence
* Having a positive opinion about oneself
* Knowing one's strengths and weaknesses
* Good sense of humor
* Ability to know others
* Perseverance and retaining of hope in times of difficulties and uncertainties
* Learning from one's experiences
* Employing one's intelligence and ingenuity, and using broad-mindedness
* Having an ability to isolate oneself from a chaotic environment

A setback in one's life does not have to mean that one is doomed forever. It can serve as a turning point in one's life toward success.

BY leading a meaningless life, poison of hopelessness gradually permeates into one's heart and mind. An effective antidote to this poison of despondence is to think of Allah (God). For the person feeling close to Allah, life at once becomes purposeful and majestically meaningful. Anyone, who holds Allah in one's memory indelibly, is ultimately always a winner in the game of life despite facing an apparent failure. Without this element in one's life, in spite of achieving all the worldly successes and looking like a winner, one is bound to be a loser in the final determination.

DECISION MAKING

How easy or difficult making of a decision can be depends on the situation at hand. For example, a man said to his buddy, "For me, I have to take my wife for a dinner out or to a movie every time before she would agree to my coming here to play golf, how do you manage to get here"? His friend replied, "You are spending so much money just for coming to golf course. I simply give my wife a definite choice to decide between two courses, and she readily lets me come to the golf course".

There may come up a time or a situation in one's life that one may not be left with any alternative of one's own choice. Under such a circumstance, it is not what one really wanted to do but what one had to. In such situation, if the outcome happens to be in one's best interest, one cannot be given a credit for it because this was not the outcome of one's own decision.

Having to make a decision is one of the causes of anxiety. Any major decision, particularly the one that would affect many lives has to be made very carefully. Here, Carefully Implies:

❖ Do not make a decision based on incomplete information. That would automatically prevent your taking a wrong step in a hurry.

❖ Keep in mind that the current situation might be different (as is usually the case) from the one you have experienced in the past. Before making a final decision each situation should be considered on an individual basis.

❖ Do not let your expectations overshadow the reality, instead, try as best as possible to see the things as they are, not as they seem or you would like them to be.

❖ Do not assume that a thing has also become as clear to others as it is to you even though you might have explained it to them very clearly. That will save you from meeting surprises.

❖ Do not be overconfident. Beware of being under a false impression that the whole world is with you.

❖ Do not think that your conclusion derived from a certain statement or a statistical data has to be correct. A thing may be interpreted differently by others and their interpretation may also be as reasonable or understandable as yours.

❖ Weigh the pros and cons of your decision as much realistically as possible before carrying it out.

❖ Your opponent or enemy might not be as bad as you think. Keep open the possibility of a workable solution to come out through solemn negotiations in a friendly manner.

ART OF LIVING

Balanced rich in fiber diet, moderate exercise, e.g. walking, maintaining healthy habits, being productive, keeping oneself busy in some creative activity of one's interest, staying poised in state of anger, adversity or prosperity are a part of the art of living.

Give a smile, laugh with others, and at yourself.

Do not usurp anyone's right and do not let anyone usurp your right. Have the decency of not exploiting anyone and the prudence not to be a victim of it.

We may choose to behave in a constructive manner and strive to improve ourselves or we may adopt maladaptive behavior, e.g. substance abuse, drinking alcohol, cigarette smoking, guilty pleasures, haughtiness, pomposity, or extravagance. Islam permits enjoying worldly luxuries but not extravagance (7: 31)

Art of Living lies in making a rule TO:

- ❖ Exercise patience and self-control
- ❖ Call for what is right
- ❖ Turn away from those who decline to understand
- ❖ Turn to Allah only on facing any provocation or opposition

(Reference, Al-Qur'an: **7**: 146, 199 to 201; **31**: 18, 19)

ART OF BETTER LIVING

People have different goals to achieve. Anything one may devotedly choose to attain and maintain would be one's value. A list of personal values can be much longer but some common personal values that people may have ARE:

Happiness, Prosperity, Academic Education, Health, Family, Fame, Homeland, Hobby.

One of integrity, would under all circumstances stay consistent with the self-established principles whether admirable or not. Thus, a person of integrity may or may not be honest but would have no conflict regarding his/her values.

Most admirable, Universal (Moral, Natural) Human Values ARE:

Truthfulness, Patience, Fairness, Honesty, Modesty, Kindness, Generosity, Sincerity.

The art of better living is to obtain personal goals while keeping the Natural Human Values, i.e. to earn by fair means. In other words, to achieve success by hook, not by crook.

Performing the deeds of righteousness, i.e. being polite, respectful and helpful to everyone especially to one's parents, relatives, orphans or wayfarers AND refraining from evil deeds (lying, backbiting, stealing, killing, indecent or unhealthy practices) is the basic standard of one's leading a modest, moderate, decent life. Adding God to it, would make one religious, otherwise one would be secular. Secularism would be comparable to fulfilling the child's all material needs but keeping him/her deprived of the element of love. A righteous atheist would be moral but not spiritual.

God is in everyone's DNA. God has built WiFi and installed the free "Godmail" app. in every individual but one has to connect and activate it. AL-Qur'an addresses the whole humankind and contains in it full guidance as to how one should conduct self in one's day-to-day life. "If men be good, government cannot be bad".

SUCCESSFUL LIFE

This life of ours is a Test. It may be compared to a game, not play. The difference between game and play is, that in case of latter, one may do anything that one may like without being held responsible for one's actions, but the former has its set rules and regulations, and it ties in a sense of responsibility or accountability to it. Thus, one may make it or may come out as a loser.

Real success is that one achieves by strictly adhering to the natural human values. Set any goals that you want to accomplish in your life and then start working to achieve them without violating the natural human values. The higher you set your goals and accomplish them in keeping with the universal moral values the higher the level of your achievement and more successful your life would be.

DO YOUR BEST AT DOING GOOD
HOPE FOR THE BEST
BE PREPARED FOR THE WORST
AS BEST AS FEASIBLE

SUBTLE BUT SIGNIFICANT

❖ Patience is going by reason rather than by emotion. It is not cool-heartedness.

❖ Patience is exercising control on one's emotions, temptations or desires, and forbearance of stressful situations of life. It is not toleration of brutality or injustice.

❖ Nobility is being steadfast on natural human values. It is not cowardice.

❖ Civility is being kind to others. It is not weakness.

❖ Honesty is the best policy. It is not stupidity.

❖ Modesty is a virtue. It is not timidity.

❖ Firmness is taking a stand on what is right. It is not obstinacy.

❖ Assertion is claiming one's legitimate right. It is not aggression.

❖ Warning is to caution. It is not insulting.

❖ Pride is being confident of one's achievements or faculties. It is not egoism, arrogance, or bragging of one's achievements.

❖ Taking adequate needed rest is essential for health. It is not laziness.

❖ Convincing is to persuade someone to believe in truth. It is not to impose, force or to coerce.

MUSIC

Music, the "Universal Language", is a form of nonverbal communication. It has its roots in the human's desire to express that goes beyond words. Any external manifestation of it is not necessary for the appreciation of music. After birth, the first melody that a baby comes to feel is that of his mother's voice. Music, in an unconscious manner, has an impact on heart and brain. Through music, we can get a picture of a person's inner emotional state, e.g. one might be impatiently and powerfully thumping on the drums producing noise rather than music while another might be playing on violin, "twinkle, twinkle little star". The latter, most likely would be, within self, calm and poised, and the former, highly anxious, angry, aggressive and unable to concentrate.

Music listening demands attention. "Music with dinner is an insult both to the cook and the violinist". Generally, a pleasant tune produces a relaxing effect. A well-balanced combination of the elements of music (tune, rhythm, melody and color) can enhance one's imagination and make one more susceptible to exciting stimuli. In such a state, music lover would feel tired after a longer time. However, the same type of music can have a different effect on different individuals that would be unpredictable. It also depends on the type of music, circumstances and mindset of the person at the time. Music has an effect on human's pulse rate, blood pressure, blood circulation, rate of breathing and glandular secretions, Like, weather and light, sound also has an impact on human emotions.

In children, music helps develop areas of the brain for later academic tasks such as reading and mathematics. Early musical experiences dramatically enhance a child's ability to acquire language, vocabulary, logic, spatial reasoning, sensory-motor skills, and rhythmic skills.

We do not throw away the entire mail we just discard the junk mail. It would be advisable to avoid junk food or contaminated food rather than to eliminate all food and decide to live only on air and enriched water. All music is not junk music nakedness is not an ingredient of music.

Prophet Muhammad peace be upon him had suggested that, one with the most beautiful voice should render the Az'an (call for the Sal'at Prayer). If piano be removed from the Church there would definitely occur some deficiency, call it whatever you may like to. There is a built-in element of music in the Text of the Holy Qur'an as a beautiful recitation of it unmistakably indicates. A heart-touching recitation of the Holy Qur'an, in my experience, is the finest of music.

BEAUTY

Beauty is a special grace or charm.

Each component of everything existing in Nature carries a built-in element of beauty regardless of whether we see it or not.

Beauty is any of those qualities of objects, sounds, emotional or intellectual concepts, behavior etc. that gratify or arouse admiration to a high degree especially by the perfection of form resulting from the harmonious combination of diverse elements in unity.

Beauty is the name of a combination of and a proper ratio of the elements in anything along with its being of benefit.

Beauty is a combination of qualities that pleases the aesthetic senses, intellect or moral sense.

Beautiful-looking things are not always good but good things are always beautiful.

Goodness is beauty. A good character is beautiful. Allah (G0d) created beauty in things and instilled in human the capability of appreciating it, searching it, benefiting from it, enjoying it, and being thankful to the Creator for everything.

- ❖ Enjoying a thing means, feeling pleased by and/or benefitting from it.
- ❖ It is not necessary to understand the mechanics or mechanism of action of a thing in order to enjoy it.

STAGES TO KNOWLEDGE

"Ignorance is the curse of God. Knowledge, the wing wherewith we fly to heaven". Like curiosity, doubt can also be useful in acquiring knowledge.

There are six stages to knowledge:

- ❖ Asking questions in a good manner
- ❖ Remaining quiet and listening attentively
- ❖ Understanding well
- ❖ Memorizing
- ❖ Teaching
- ❖ Acting upon the knowledge and keeping to its limits

Knowledge comprises the information of all fields, such as sciences dealing with matter and energy, life sciences, economics, sociology, anthropology, arts, culture, psychology, philosophy and religion. "Unity of Knowledge" may be likened to a tree giving out diverse offshoots. It is like an umbrella encompassing all the subjects. By looking at only one piece of puzzle we cannot see the whole picture. Just as a drop of water cannot be called an ocean, nonetheless, it cannot be denied as being a part of the ocean. Likewise, a small bit of information may not be considered knowledge but still it would be a part of knowledge, albeit a very tiny one. One person may get totally absorbed into a single drop of water while another may not pay much attention to the entire ocean. However, "None is so blind who Will not see".

ART AND SCIENCE

Some people give little importance to subjects like art, philosophy, religion, etc. because they consider them mere products of human mind. They find them of no material value, hence not worth their attention. However, any researcher who sternly disregards the possibility of significance of everything that is not detected by any of the human five senses, is certainly a reductionist, if not a pseudo-scientist. Let us not forget that mathematics, universally established as the most exact science known to human, is purely a product of human mind. Amazingly enough, even in mathematics, quite often the process of calculation starts after making a supposition of some number or letter. Someone, regarding mathematics, had said to me, "Well, how can you expect to come up with something really true that has been derived from your own supposition to start with". In spite of that, it would be foolish to cast aside the subject of mathematics.

It would pay to keep in mind that the things appearing rational at first sight may not be so, and vice versa. A truly progressive scientist remains mentally receptive to each possibility, weighs all the variables systematically, makes use of more and more advanced instruments, and endeavors to make intangibles, tangible.

A true scientist would not ignore or let go of anything simply because it seems to be just a product of mind. Things, labelled as products of human mind, are not all meaningless. They may be logical, rational OR illogical, irrational. It would be a serious mistake to discard a logical human thought just by saying that such things are nothing more than the products of human mind, and therefore, spending any time, energy or money in the study of such useless intangible conjectures would be a solemn-sounding waste.

IS GOD MAN-MADE?

God made man or man made God? One idea is that man needed some superhuman entity to turn to at the time of trouble or adversity. Some believe that man could not accept his permanent death and therefore, out of his need to give some meaning to his life, man invented the idea of life after death. Their saying is, that there is no God and the plain fact is that everything in the universe is purposeless, but some wretched, weak-hearted persons cannot face this naked reality. However, before we accept this as the last word in the story of human life, let us take a view of the other side of the argument too.

Rene Descartes had tried to prove his own existence by saying, "I think, therefore I am". However things do exist even without their being able to think. This ability to think requires to being set into the system, mere existence of a thing does not automatically imply its ability to think also. A radio can receive signals, a make-up box cannot. We know that we are free to choose between what to eat and what not to eat. We also have the freedom of making a choice to eat or not to eat. But we are not free to have no appetite to eat. This built-in hunger for food is neither a chance development nor purposeless. Even the freedom to decide, to eat or not to eat has been given to us. It is not a chance that we yearn to find God, this desire of ours, like our appetite to eat, has also been installed in our system. We are free to choose to believe or not to believe but we are not free to have no desire to believe. Man's urge to know himself, to know his Creator, to find out his fate in life leads him to study Nature. The discoveries made by the man in the zeal of satisfying this quest of his are the byproducts of his search. But when, despite achieving material success, this basic thirst remains unquenched, then the genuine human searcher, instead of defeatedly lowering the standard, continues to strive for achievement of the ultimate goal. God has instilled this flame of desire into our system. It would have been very unfair to us For God to expect us to have a belief in God and not to give us the necessary desire and capacity to do so. The very fact that we have a desire to know our Creator indicates that there is ONE!

It would also be unfair to us for God to expect from us that we must conduct ourselves in a certain manner and not to provide us any guidance to it. Our stay on the Earth, at individual level, compared to the time span of whole human existence on the Earth would probably be less than a second. This situation is proportionally far worse than being in an ongoing three-hour conference for thirty seconds only. So, if there is any Creator, Who really cares for us, then we cannot be left in chaos to make blind guesses about our destiny, and then out of disappointment, lose all faith in life. We have to be informed. We must be informed at least a little bit of what it is all about, and what is expected of us before we can be held responsible for our actions. We have to have the Guidance. We have a right to know.

God has surely, furnished humankind with the necessary guidance from time to time, the last one being the Holy Qur'an revealed to Prophet Muhammad peace be upon him. Those, who think that The Qur'an is outdated will not find any such principles in this Book that cannot be appropriately applied in modern life.

God did not leave us relying entirely on our common sense because things based on our common sense alone may or may not be true, for example, at one time, the Earth was understood to be flat and stationary. God provided us the axioms to direct our God-given common sense to use it in a discrete manner, and be able to win laurels here as well as in the Hereafter.

We look at the Empire State Building and we know that it is man-made. We look at a weaver-bird's nest and we know that it is not man-made. What I am trying to say that we should first understand that everything has been created, if not by man, by some other agency, and then try to make a concept of there being an Ultimate Creator of All.

God has given the human mind the faculties to think, to reason, and to decide. Man manufactured mirrors, invented television, computers, jets, designed robots, and even has carried out the miraculous cloning, but the basic raw material in all human creations is never man-made. God created the raw material and then gave it different forms and from them, shaped the whole universe without any previously existing design or model of it.

Even the atheists believe that the source of the origin of the universe is some kind of ethereal Energy. And, a part of that Energy, under certain environmental conditions, over a long, long period of time, got transformed into manifold levels of density, eg. X-rays, light rays, sound waves, gases, liquids and solids. And then, through some chemical processes and physical forces, various planets came into existence and started revolving. And then, on Earth, under some specially suitable circumstances, there happened to develop life, first in the form of a single cell or some bacteria. And then, from a single cell started the whole chain of life that has led to the evolvement of an immense variety and innumerable forms of it. For example, algae, orchids, pitcher plants, apples, pineapples, flamingoes, butterflies, fireflies, eagles, whooping cranes, corals, goldfish, dolphins, whales, reptiles, ants, elephants, cows, deer, dinosaurs, chimpanzees and even man. And all that had taken place through an automatic evolutionary process. Intelligence also happened to develop automatically, and as it played a vital role in the process of natural selection and survival of the fittest, this trait got gradually strengthened, genetically. This approach suggests that the afore-mentioned Energy, without any intelligent organization, has produced all the manifestations as a result of totally unplanned or self-regulating evolutionary process in which human conscience has also been a chance development.

The other view is, that there is likely to be some intelligence behind the afore-said Energy which, through a designed engineering, has brought about all manifestations in a planned evolutionary process. This means that creation of the universe is intentional and with a purpose.

RADICALS OF PERSON

Food, sex, clothing and shelter are not the radicals of person but are the major driving forces of a person. Body and Soul can be regarded as two major radicals of Person. Existence of human body is obvious but soul is so elusive that scientists are not sure of its being a reality. Mind is the function of brain but it also has escaped a satisfactory definition. Hence, science has limited itself to the study of body and behavior physiology deals with the former and psychology with the latter.

Human brain is also a highly complex organ but at least it is physically there to be studied through various techniques, e.g. x-ray, scanning and MRI (magnetic resonance imaging. PET (positron emission tomography) is a special imaging technique to measure live changes in various areas of the brain.

Stem Cell is the precursor of all body cells. In other words, stem cell has the potential of developing into any organ of the body. DNA may be considered as the single most radical of person. We may expand it to create a bio-psycho-socio-spiritual model representing the four basic radicals or aspects of person. Since a person is much more than the sum of its parts, study of person can lead us into a myriad of radicals or elements related to person, e.g. health, wealth, fame, happiness, education, character, conscience, fairness, integrity, sincerity, honesty, reality testing, reasoning, understanding, sharing, courage, wisdom, faith, hope, peace of mind. Going into the emotional radicals of person can be staggering, e.g. love, anger, jealousy, greed, etc.

SPIRITUALITY

Yearning for a feeling of peace and tranquility in being close to, and being in harmony with the Almighty Superpower is, Spirituality. Call it Allah, God or by whatever Name it would ultimately come to the same One, Creator and Sustainer of the Universes.

Since eternity, human has felt a desire to believe in some Super-human-power, and has made sacrifices of one kind or the other in Its name. This indicates or at least suggests that a desire to believe in some Superpower is a built-in feature into the human nature. This desire of human being is actually a spiritual human need that also demands its fulfillment.

Study of skies and the earth and of everything (living, non-living, solids, liquids, gases, raws, etc.) in between them shows an organized pattern and a perfectly balanced harmonious interrelationship of things with one another. One may wonder whether all that has become about by mere chance or there does exist a meaningful planning behind it. Man's urge to know himself, to know his Creator, to find out his fate in life leads him to study Nature.

NATURE STUDY

There is so much complexity and organization even in the simplest things in Nature, that it is difficult for me to believe that universe is an outcome of an unplanned scheme. The formation of DNA, messenger RNA, transfer RNA, ribosomal RNA, and the processes of transcription and translation leading to synthesis of specific proteins and hormones point to their being more than chance occurrences. To me, a disciplined organization, as observed in ants, bees, migratory birds, etc., is more than a random phenomenon. We do see many things seemingly happening automatically on their own, e.g. alternation of day and night, but that can be deceptive. For example, when we see things happening automatically in a big factory, we know that neither the factory came into existence by some chance nor the things in it started happening on their own as a result of some haphazard activity that in some strange manner had become thus organized. I am not sure if more examples would make my presentation any more meaningful. I suppose, for a wise person, enough is enough. (This reminds me of: When the Judge asked an 85 YR old wife seeking divorce from her 87 YR old husband after their having been together for more than sixty years, "Why now", her response was, "enough is enough").

Al-Qur'an: **55:** 19 to 21 say, "Allah has let free two bodies of flowing water, meeting together, between them is a barrier that they do not transgress. Then which of the favors of your Lord will you deny".

ALLAH did create Human out of an extract of clay. Then Allah placed human as a "nutfa" (fertilized ovum) in a safe lodging, firmly fixed, then Allah turned the nutfa into a leech-like form, and then Allah gave it a form of a lump (foetus), then out of that lump Allah made bones, then clothed the bones with flesh, and then Allah brought it forth as *another* creation (i.e. *human* as differentiated from animals). So blessed be Allah, the Best of Creators (Al-Qur'an: **22: 5**).

❖ Mostly, the parasites do bring about some harm to their host. However, cuscuta is a parasitic plant that is smart enough to derive all of its nourishment from its host tree without causing any kind of harm to the tree. The lesson to learn here is, that, at least, one should not be in any way detrimental to the society that one is benefitting from.

❖ Kangaroo is famous for its hopping gait. Studies have shown that in this way less energy is used as compared to what would be required for a normal four-legged walk. One difference between a wise and a not so wise person is that the former accomplishes the same task by spending relatively less energy.

❖ The male bowerbird builds on the ground a bower (open house, hut, apartment, private chamber) in which to display itself to attract the female. The bower has a floor of twigs, its sides lean together to form a roof and it is open on both sides. Bowerbird decorates the hut with bright "ornaments" such as shells, feathers and flowers. It also paints the apartment with fruit pulp by a spongy brush of fiber (wad) retained in the bill. The bower is oriented north south so that the bird is not dazzled by the sun while displaying. The male bird may display for several months posturing with the display objects held in the bill until, with the seasonal appearance of insect food for the young, mating takes place in the private chamber (bower).

Al-Qur'an: **6: 38** says, "There is neither an animal on the earth nor a being that flies on its wings but forms communities like you. WE did not neglect anything in the Book, then, to their Lord they will be gathered".

STUDY of ants has revealed some amazing findings. For Example:

- ❖ Ants bury their dead in a manner similar to humans.
- ❖ Ants have a sophisticated system of division of labor whereby they have, Managers, Supervisors, Foremen, Workers, etc.
- ❖ Ants hold meetings among themselves to have a chat.
- ❖ Ants hold regular markets wherein they exchange goods.
- ❖ Ants have an advanced method of communication among themselves.
- ❖ Ants store grain for long periods in winter and if the grain begins to bud, they cut its roots as if they understand that if they leave it to grow, it will rot.
- ❖ If the grains they have stored would get wet due to rain they take those grains out into the sunlight to dry, and once those are dry they take them back inside as if they know that humidity will cause development of root system and thereafter, rotting of the grain.
- ❖ One kind of migratory bird makes a return flight of thousands of miles by forming a symmetrical figure of "8". This is because of a complex programming set into its system. Point to ponder is, WHO did all that programming and was it essential for the survival of this particular species?

"And hark! How blithe the throstle sings!
He too is no mean preacher
Come forth into the light of things
Let Nature be your teacher"
(William Wordsworth)

"One touch of Nature makes the whole world kin"
(William Shakespeare)

"Never does Nature say one thing and wisdom another".

"The study of nature is the intercourse with the Highest Mind. You should never trifle with Nature".

The Holy Qur'an is for us a Reminder, a book of Guidance for us to follow and of Signs for us to reflect upon.

A Muslim scientist would be at least one step ahead of others because whatever is given in the Holy Qur'an is already an established fact (axiom) for him and he will take on from there.

"Science without religion is lame; religion without science is blind" (Albert Einstein).

"Reason is a light that God has kindled in the soul" (Aristotle).

Obedience to God (Islam) is a universal religion. For humans, it started with the creation of Adam and Eve. Allah has sent a prophet to each nation, some followed their prophet, and some didn't. They all preached: Pray to One God only, perform righteous deeds and stay away from evil things, and disregard those who would differ. In this regard, primitive religions are the grossest deviations from the original religion rather than origin of the religion.

"None is so blind who WILL not see", Jesus Christ peace be upon him said.
"God offers to every mind its choice between truth and repose.
Take which you please - you can never have both".
(Ralph Waldo Emerson).

MY MUSLIM IDENTITY

I have been for a good number of years in Pakistan and also in America. In both countries, in general, I have been treated well at all levels, but not by all. Irritating experiences have also been a part of my life. Anyone who has seen the seasons, in terms of decades, would not need any examples to be quoted to have a feel for what it is going through the vicissitudes of even a normal life.

The Ultimate Sustainer of all, Almighty Allah has always sustained me through thick and thin (one need not ask here whether me deserving or not).

I have been residing in New York City for about fifty years by now. Familiarly known as the "Big Apple" this city is also called by some a "Melting Pot". Once, a 17 Yr old doctor from India, on his TV interview, had remarked that he considered New York City like a mosaic pattern rather than a melting pot, implying thereby, that there being many different communities settled down in it as "New Yorkers" yet maintaining their own shine without losing the luster of their cultural heritage or religious identity.

In America, I have passed through a transitory phase during which i felt that it might be unwise on my part to tell everyone of my being a Muslim but now I am glad that I never yielded to that unfounded feeling of mine.

I would say that residing in a multicultural society in America with my Muslim identity has been more of a stimulating experience for me rather than a challenging one.

In Pakistan, nobody ever asked me about my views regarding Existence of God, life after death, reincarnation or celebrating Christmas. I have learnt that one needs to have a good grasp of the Islamic education in order to feel confident among people of diverse denominations. A Bengali doctor's standpoint was that he did believe in the presence of some kind of Energy because no process could ever start from a state of total nothingness, implausible for him, he said, was to believe in heaven and Hell type of things.

In my native land, moon-sight controversy had never struck me as being any serious problem. However, while residing among people of other faiths and cultures I have perceived this "knotty" point to be significant enough to render our children prone to doubt the excellence of Islam (obedience to God) and feel less comfortable of their Muslim Identity. The Qur'anic Verses, **10:** 5 and **17:** 12 clearly tell us about the precisely set stages of moon and sun to help us formulate a Calendar. Many Verses of the Holy Qur'an are an open invitation to the human to study the universe, develop mathematical skills, discover and invent things and make scientific progresses. This also shows that need to understand Islam is by the study the Holy Qur'an rather from the behavior of those who would not be going along with its Guidance.

The Holy Qur'an's guidance is to treat all people justly and kindly regardless of their ethnic or religious background, and we may do business with them. Allah forbids us to befriend only those particular individuals (not the whole class) who fought with us on account of religion, who drove us out of our homes or helped to drive us out of our homes (AL-Qur'an: **60:** 8, 9).

My impression is that there are many who are uninformed or misinformed about Islam. As, Muslims, it is our duty to represent Islam by our actions and then spreading the word around. From time to time, I have been asked questions regarding Fasting, Hajj, capital punishment, polygamy, alcohol and so on. It must be realized that for imparting true to form Islamic information to others one needs to adequately explain it to them.

Superficially looking at it polygamy, appears to be unfair but it needs to be understood in light of the conditions in which it is permitted in Islam. By keeping in view the astonishing complexities of human life and being given the situation of women exceeding the number of men in the society, it would not be difficult to understand the legitimacy of polygamy. This permission in the Law is tightly laced with a persistent demand on the husband to be fair to his wives.

A woman's share in the heirship being half of the man's seems like usurping the rights of women. First of all, this guidance is to be applied in the absence of the Will. In practical sense, it is fair because, in Islam, woman is not obliged to earn livelihood for herself or provide financial support to the family. Nevertheless, she is not barred from working outside the home if no domestic disharmony or child neglect is being caused by it.

In case of being a witness, a woman in islam is not considered less credible than a man. Presence of a second woman is required for mere support (ours is a male dominant society). In case one forgets the other one may remind her, man can also forget but is not given this privilege.

Islam distinctly discourages divorce but recognizes that a situation can be where it may be the only solution. In Islam, both men and women, have the right to obtain divorce and to remarry. Needless to say, that, men and women have equal rights as human beings but the natural biological differences between men and women have to be given their proper regard and Islam is appropriately regardful of this living reality. Like integrity and honesty, Equality and fairness are two different things. Distribution of wealth in Islam is based on justice, not equality.

Plunging into debates whether or not capital punishment is an effective measure to eliminate crime from the society is actually evading the matter. The real issue is whether to take the criminal to task in a just manner, or not.

Had Islam spread through sword, then the parents in succeeding generations would not have continued to be so keen to instil the spirit of Islam into their children. This shows the inherent goodness of Islam, and the appreciation by the parents of its vital necessity in life. Dividing the religion, making false allegations, pre/extra marital sex, gambling, alcohol or substance abuse, or usury systems have no place in Islam.

Islam requires one to be objective and not to get affected by rumors. Spying in social life is not in accordance with Islamic way of life. Islamic teaching is to deal honestly. Islam promotes justice which is a prerequisite to establishing peace.

Living among people of different faiths and cultures is a good opportunity to observe common points between Islam and other disciplines. It also provides precious chances to get across to others the Islamic point of view of things.

Islam cultivates an atmosphere of understanding among people. I remember, one day, a mentally disturbed patient came to my office. As I said, "Good afternoon", he precipitately retorted, "What is good about it". He appeared at the time very hostile and very liable to be destructive. Then I said to him, "I mean to say peace be upon you". In double-quick time, he turned calm and cooperative. The whole change of scene was dramatic. Later, I talked about that happening to a Jewish doctor and a Korean doctor who also worked there. When I asked them if they knew or could think of any better way of greeting someone than offered by Islam, their reply was, No". Islamic way is trying to be first to greet others by saying, "AsSalamo-alay-Kum", meaning, "Peace be upon you", and to give a better or at least an equivalent response to other person's greetings to you regardless of the other person being a Muslim or not.

In my childhood, I was taught that Islam is the best religion. Now, out of my own experience of residing in a multicultural society, I would affirm that Islam is a way of life to be proudest of. Islam means, obedience to God.

- ❖ Nothing can develop or no one can develop anything without there being present a potential of that.
- ❖ There is no need to forbid a thing if there would be no one having a potential to carry it out.

FINEST OF STORIES

Prophet Yaqoob (Jacob) was grandson of Prophet Ibraheem (Abraham) and son of Prophet Ish'aq (Issac) peace be upon them all and had settled in Hebron (Palestine). Including Yusuf (Joseph), he had twelve sons. Among the eleven brothers of Yusuf, only Bin Yamin (Benjamin) was his full brother, the other ten were his step-brothers.

Yusuf was born in or about 1906 B.C. He grew up as a compellingly handsome boy. Among all the brothers, Yusuf and Bin Yamin were the favorites of their father but Yusuf, in particular, was the apple of his father's eyes. For this reason, his ten brothers were especially envious of him. They felt their father was not in his right mind by showing more love for Yusuf, because they thought they themselves were also a group of good ones.

Yusuf was 17 YR old when he dreamt that the *sun, moon* and *eleven stars* bowed down before him. Perplexed by his dream, the boy told his father all what he had dreamt. His father gave him a hint that someday Allah will choose him and teach him making interpretations of stories and events. However, he advised him not to relate it to his brothers, lest they concoct a plan against him.

One day, his step-brothers did decide to get rid of him in order to be the sole recipients of their father's favor. They talked seriously about slaying him or casting him out in some unknown land. They thought they have plenty of time to repent and be righteous after that. One of them stated, "If you must do something, then instead of slaying him, throw him down to the bottom of a well, may be from there some caravan of travelers might pick him up".

Then, they approached their father and said, "O our father why don't you trust us with our brother, seeing we are indeed his sincere well-wishers, send him with us tomorrow to play and enjoy himself, we shall take every care of him". Their father said, "Really, it saddens me that you take him away; I fear lest a wolf eat him up while you do not attend him".

They replied, "If a wolf were to devour him in our company, while we are such a large party, then we should indeed first have perished ourselves, if such a thing happens that would show that we are really worth nothing". Then, they took him away, and they all agreed to throw him down to the bottom of a well. During their carrying out of their plan, Yusuf felt in the heart Godly Voice: "Of a surety, you shall one day tell them the truth of this affair of theirs while they do not know you".

Then, they came to their father in the early part of the night, weeping and saying, "O our father, while we went racing with one another and left our brother with our things, a wolf devoured him. But, you will never believe us even though we tell the truth". They had stained his shirt with false blood and brought that as evidence. Their father said, "Nay, but your minds have made up a tale that may pass with you, but for me, patience is most fitting against that which you present. Only Allah's help is to be sought".

Then, there came a caravan of travelers that was, on the way back to its home - Egypt. They sent their water-carrier to fetch water. He let down his bucket into the well. To his surprise he said, "Ah there, Good News, here is a fine young man"! They concealed him as a treasure. At their first opportunity, they sold him for a miserable price - for a few Dirhams (a coin of the value of two pence) counted out. They did not expect a big price on him.

The man in Egypt, who had bought him, said to his wife, "Make his stay among us honorable; maybe he will bring us much good or we shall adopt him as our son". Thus, Allah established him in the land to teach him the interpretation of stories and events. Allah does whatever Allah wills but most people do not understand this. When Yusuf reached his full maturity, Allah gave him power and knowledge. Thus, Allah rewards those who do right.

Now, the woman in whose house he was, sought to tempt him and seduce him, and one day she closed the doors and said, "Come on, I am ready and prepared fo you"! The young man stated, "Allah forbid, truly your husband is my lord and has made my stay agreeable, I will not play on him. Truly no good come those who do wrong". However, with passion she desired him and advanced towards him. He would have advanced towards her, had he not perceived his Lord's inspiration appealing to his conscience, i.e. it was not worthy of him to yield to the temptation by the woman. Thus, Allah turned him away from indecency and immodesty for he was one of Allah's sincere servants.

They both raced each other. She took hold of his shirt and tore it by pulling it. Suddenly, they met her husband near the door. She, at once said, "What is the fitting punishment for one who formed an evil design against your wife, but prison or painful torment"? Yusuf said, "It was she that sought to seduce me, from my true self". The husband, who was a prominent person in the town, was quite puzzled at all that.

At that, a female member of the family mentioned a circumstantial evidence, saying, "If it be that his shirt is torn from the front, then her tale is true and he is a liar, but if it be that his shirt is torn from the back, then she is the liar and he is speaking the truth". When her husband saw his shirt torn from the back, he remarked, "Behold, it is a plot of you women, certainly mighty is your snare". To Yusuf he said, "O Yusuf, leave this matter". To his wife he said, "Beg forgiveness for your sin, for truly you have been at fault".

That news spread in the town like wildfire and the women in the city said, "The wife of the great Aziz is seeking to lure her slave for she has passionately fallen in love with him; we see she is evidently going astray". When she heard of their malicious talk, she invited them to a banquet at her house and gave each of them a knife, and called the young man to come out before them. Then, as they caught sight of Yusuf, they were amazed at his beauty and in their astonishment, cut their hands. They said, "Good God, No mortal is this, he is indeed a noble angel". Then, she said to the women, "This is he, the young man, about whom you did blame me for his love, I did seek to attract him but he escaped and now, if he does not yield to my bidding he shall certainly be cast into prison and will be humbled and disgraced".

The young man, finding himself hoodwinked, prayed to Allah, "O my Lord, prison is more to my liking than that which they invite me to. Unless you ward off from me their cunning devices, I might in my youthful folly, feel inclined toward them and join the rank of the ignorant". Allah granted his prayer and warded off from him their snare.

Then, it occurred to the men, despite having seen the signs, that it would be best to imprison Yusuf for a time. Now, with him, there came in the prison two young men. One day, one of them said, "I saw myself in a dream, pressing wine". The other man said, "I saw myself, in a dream, carrying bread on my head and birds were eating thereof". "Inform us of the interpretation of our dreams for we see you are one of the good-doers". Yusuf (now, Prophet Yusuf peace be upon him) said, "No food will come to you as your provision but I shall inform you of its interpretation before the food comes to you. This ability of interpreting dreams is a part of what my Lord has taught me. Verily, I have abandoned the religion of a people that believe not in Allah and deny the Hereafter. I have followed the religion of my fathers, Abraham, Isaac and jacob (peace be upon them all, prophets). It is not for us that we attribute any partners to Allah, this is from the Grace of Allah to us and to humankind but most people think not. O, my two companions of the prison, are many different lords better or Allah the One, Irresistible? You worship not besides Allah but only names that you have fabricated for which Allah sent no authority to you and to your fathers. Allah has commanded that you worship none but Allah only, that is the religion, straight but most people know not. O two companions, as for one of you, he will serve wine for his lord. As for the other, he will meet crucifixion and birds will eat off his head. Thus, has this matter been decreed concerning which, you both did inquire."

Then, to the one he considered would be released, Prophet Yusuf pbuh said, "You do mention me to your Lord". It came out that the same one, after his release, was appointed as a servant to the king of Egypt to pour out wine for him but he became neglectful and Satan made him completely forget to mention the young man in the prison to his lord. Consequently, Prophet Yusuf pbuh lingered in the prison for a few more years.

One day, the king of Egypt had a dream. He said, "I saw in a dream seven fat cows which seven lean ones were devouring and seven green ears of corn and seven withered ones. O you chiefs, explain to me my dream if it be that you can interpret dreams". They answered, "These are mixed up false dreams and we are not skilled in the interpretation of dreams". Then, the man released from the prison and now a servant to the king, suddenly remembered and said, "I will tell you the interpretation of this dream, you send me forth to the prison".

There, he addressed Prophet Yusuf pbuh, "O the man of truth, tell me the meaning of the dream of, seven fat cows which seven lean cows are devouring and of seven green ears of corn and seven dry ones, that I may return to the people and that they may know". Prophet Yusuf pbuh said, "You shall sow as usual for seven years, and that which you reap so you shall save it by leaving it in ears except a little of that you may eat. Then will come after that a period of seven hard years, which will devour that you shall have saved in advance, all except a little that you shall have specially guarded, for seeds. Then will come after that a year in which people will have abundant rainfall and in which they will press juice and oil."

Thus, the king learnt from the interpretation of the dream that, a terrible famine was to follow after seven years that would last for seven years, and how to prepare for it during the coming seven years. The king said, "You bring that man to me". When the messenger came to the prison and delivered the king's message, Prophet Yusuf said, "You go back to your lord and ask him - first to find out the truth about those women who had cut their hands, so far my Sustainer alone is aware of that trap".

Thereupon, the king sent for those women and when they came he asked, "What was it that you hoped to achieve when you sought to make Yusuf yield himself unto you"? The women answered, "God save us we did not perceive the least evil intention on his part". The wife of Aziz said, "Now, the truth is manifest to all, it was I who sought to make him yield unto me, whereas he, behold, was speaking the truth".

When Prophet Yusuf pbuh learned what had happened, he said, "I had asked for this so that Aziz might know that I did not betray him behind his back, and that Allah does not bless with Guidance the artful schemes of those who betray their trust. Yet I am not trying to absolve myself for verily man's innerself does incite him to evil. The human soul is certainly prone to evil unless my Sustainer bestows Mercy. Behold, surely, my Sustainer is Oft-Forgiving, Most Merciful."

The king said, "Bring him to me, so that I may attach him to my own person". Then, the king spoke to Prophet Yusuf pbuh and told him, "Be assured this day you are before your own presence with rank firmly established and fidelity fully proved". Prophet Yusuf pbuh said, "Set me over the store-houses of the land under my trust, I know their importance and how to guard them and also possess knowledge".

Thus, Allah gave established power to Prophet Yusuf pbuh in the land to take possession therein as where and when he pleased. Allah guarantees the reward of those, who do good but the reward of the HereAfter is the best for those who believe and are constant in right manner.

When the famine did take over brothers of Prophet Yusuf pbuh traveled to Egypt to pick up the food grain. As soon as they came before him, he recognized them but they did not. After furnishing them forth with provisions suitable for them and they had delivered their stock-in-trade and were ready to leave, he said to them, "Bring me the brother you have of the same father but a different mother. Do you not see that I pay out full measure and that I do provide the best hospitality"? He added, "If you do not bring him to me you shall have no measure of corn from me, and you will have no permission to approach me". They said, "We shall do all we can to persuade his father to send him with us, indeed we shall". Prophet Yusuf pbuh said to his servants, "Put their traded goods back into their saddlebags secretly so that they may appreciate this when they go back to their family and be eager to return".

Then, on their return to their father, they said, "O our father, no more measure of grain shall we get unless we take our brother with us, send our brother with us so that we may get our measure and we will indeed take care of him". Their father said, "Shall I trust you with him with any result other than when I trusted you with his brother aforetime? But Allah is the best to take care of him". Then, as they opened their baggage, they found their barter returned to them. They said, "O our father, what more can we desire, here we have our stock-in-trade returned to us we shall get more food for our family. We shall take care of our brother and at the same time add a full camel's load of grain to our provisions this is but a small quantity."

Their father said, "Never will I Send Bin Yamin with you until you swear a solemn oath to me in Allah's Name that you will be sure to bring him back to me unless you are yourselves hemmed in and, powerless". When they had sworn their solemn oath, their father said, "Over all that we say, be Allah the Witness and Guardian, O my sons, enter not the capital of Egypt, all of you by one gate, you enter by different gates, not that I can profit you anything against Allah with my advice, none can command except Allah".

When they entered through different gates as their father had advised it did not profit them in the least against the Plan of Allah. It was but a necessity of their father's soul that he had discharged. He had done his best to avert the fear he had in his heart. He possessed knowledge what Allah had taught him but most people do not understand the reality of the matter.

Then, as they came into the presence of Prophet Yusuf pbuh he drew his full brother alone to himself and said to him, "I am indeed the same your own brother, now you need not grieve for what they have done". At length, when he had finished them he put his cup into his full brother's saddlebag. As they set on their journey back to home, a carrier shouted, "O you in the caravan, behold you are thieves, without doubt". Turning toward them, they asked, "What is it that you miss"? The royal servants said, "We miss the great beaker of the king, for him, who produces it is the reward of a camel-load of corn, I guarantee this", their headman added. The brothers said, "By Allah, you know well that we did not come to make mischief in the land, and we are no thieves". The Egyptians said, "What then shall be the penalty of this if you are proved to have lied"? They said, "The penalty should be that he, in whose saddlebag it is found should be held as bondman to atone for the crime, thus it is we punish the wrongdoers".

Prophet Yusuf pbuh began to search their luggage before he came to the baggage of his full brother (Bin Yamin). At length, he brought it out of Bin Yamin's baggage. Thus did Allah plan for Prophet Yusuf pbuh since he could not take his brother by the Law of the King of Egypt except, that Allah willed it. Allah raises one to degrees of wisdom whom Allah pleases, but overall, All-Knowing is Allah alone. At that discovery, the brothers remarked, "There is nothing strange in it that he has committed a theft, for there was a brother of his who also stole before him". Prophet Yusuf pbuh kept those things locked in his heart, revealing not the secret to them. He simply said to himself in an undertone - you are the worst situated. Allah knows best the truth about what you are accusing me of. Then, they said, "O exalted one, behold, he has a father aged and respected who will grieve for him, take one of us in his place, for we see that you are gracious, a good-doer". Prophet Yusuf pbuh "Allah forbid, that we take any other than him with whom we have found our property, for if we do this we shall be unjust".

When they saw no hope of his yielding, they held a conference in private. The leader among them said, "Don't you know that your father took a solemn oath from you in Allah's Name and how before this you failed in your duty in regards to your brother, Yusuf? Therefore, I will not leave this land until my father permits me to or Allah decides in my favor, for Allah is the best of all who decide. You go back to your father and say, Dear father, your son committed a theft, we did not see him stealing, we bear witness only to what we have come to know and we could not well guard against the unseen. Ask in the town, where we have been and the caravan in which we returned and you will find that we are indeed telling the truth."

Then, they told their father all that. On hearing the story, the father said, "Your souls have contrived a story good enough for you, well, I will patiently bear this one too with a good grace, maybe, Allah will bring them all back to me in the end, for Allah knows everything and all works of Allah are based on wisdom". He then turned his face away from them and cried, "How great is my grief for my son Yusuf already". He fell into silent melancholy, his eyes became white he had lost his eyesight due to suppressed sorrow. The sons exclaimed, "By Allah, never will you cease to remember Yusuf and his brother until you ruin your health or reach the last extremity of illness, or until you die". The father replied, "I moan and groan, to Allah alone, of my anguish and sorrow, I know from Allah what you know not, O my sons, you go and search for both of your brothers. And never give up hope of Allah's soothing Mercy, truly no one despairs of Allah's Mercy except those who have no faith."

They, once again set forth for Egypt. When they presented themselves before Prophet Yusuf pbuh they humbly said, "Exalted Sir, a hard time has hit us, our family and we are in great distress, though we have been able to bring a poor capital for barter, please give us full measure of grain and be charitable to us, for Allah does reward the charitable". At that Prophet Yusuf pbuh who could contain self no longer exclaimed, "Do you know what you did with Yusuf and his brother when you were ignorant"? That took them by surprise and they cried, "Are you indeed Yusuf"? The reply they received was, "Yes, I am Yusuf and here is my brother, Allah has been indeed Gracious to us, verily, those who are righteous and practice piety and abstain from sins and evil deeds and observe patience then surely Allah makes not the reward of the good-doers to be lost". They said, "By Allah, Allah has exalted you above us and we certainly have been sinners". Prophet Yusuf pbuh said, "Today, no penalty shall be inflicted on you, may Allah forgive you, Allah is the Most Merciful of all, you go with the shirt of mine and cast it over the face of my father and he shall recover his eyesight, and bring to me all the members of the family."

Then, as the caravan departed their father, although so far away, said, "I do indeed perceive the smell of Yusuf though you might think me to be in dotage". The people of the house answered, "By Allah, you are still suffering from your old delusion". When the bearer of the glad tidings arrived he cast the shirt over the father's face, his eyesight came back. He said, "Didn't I say to you that I know from Allah that which you know not"? The brothers exclaimed all together, "Dear father, pray to Allah for the pardon of our sins, for we have been indeed sinful". He said, "I will ask my Lord for forgiveness for you, verily, only Allah is the Oft-Forgiving, the Most Merciful".

When the whole family entered unto Prophet Yusuf pbuh he betook his parents to himself and said, "Enter Egypt, Allah-Willing, you will live in peace". After entering the town, he raised his parents to the throne and seated them along with himself. Then, all of them (father, mother and eleven sons), at the same time, courteously, *bowed* before him. He said, "Dear father, this is the interpretation of my dream wherein i had dreamt long ago that, the sun, moon and eleven stars were prostrating before me. My Lord has made it come true. Allah has been indeed good to me, Allah took me out of the prison and brought you all here to me from the desert after Satan had sown enmity between me and my brothers, my Lord fulfills the planned designs in mysterious ways, only Allah is All-Knowing, All-Wise." He continued, "My Lord, YOU have given me kingdom, taught me interpretations of dreams. YOU are the only Creator of the heavens and the earth, YOU are indeed my Protector, Helper, Supporter and Guardian in this world and in the Hereafter, cause me to die as a Muslim (the one submitting to Your Will), and join me with the righteous."

❖ Next follows a general discussion on two events of this story >

❖ SEDUCTION

(Related to the story)

"And when the news of the incident spread in the city, several women therein said, "The wife of Aziz had tried to seduce her servant and indeed she has fallen in love with him. Verily, we see that she is in manifest error" (AL-Qur'an: Verse: **12:** 30)

"When she heard of their accusation, she sent for them, prepared a banquet for them, gave each of them a knife, and said, "Come out before them". When they saw him, they did approve him enthusiastically and cut their hands. They said, "Allah preserve us, No man is this. This is none other than a noble angel" (Verse: **12:** 31)

- ❖ One view is that Yusuf must have been around at the time and she would have called him - come out before them - in a casual form.
- ❖ Another view is that she had specially prepared Yusuf to present him in the best form before the invited women.

Here one might wonder how come all of the invited women would cut their hands?

An explanation given to it is that Yusuf's beauty had struck all of them so much that they all happened to cut their hands in "astonishment". However, it still remains puzzling because, that an occasion that demands special attention to it would, as a rule, make one stop all activity that one might be involved in at the moment. Thus, it would be extremely unlikely that all the women present there would have kept themselves busy in cutting food even when the hostess had called Yusuf to come out before them, and then at the same time all of them happened to "accidently" cut their hands too. Possibly, Yusuf's charm had so bewitched the women that they all thought it would be their ingratitude, no less than committing a sin, on their part if they turned down that opportunity of enjoying such an angelic beauty, and as such, they cut their hands to indicate their passion for Yusuf.

Another view is that the women had cut their hands to show it to Yusuf that they were prepared to commit suicide if he would not give them the required attention. It is possible that the women might have tried adroit loving maneuvers to tickle yusuf, and that was how Yusuf had come to know that those women were also willing for him, as indicated by, "*They* invite me to" in the Verse:**12: 33**, and also by "What is the matter with the ladies that had cut their hands (Verse: **12: 50**)? In latter case, it could be that Yusuf, instead of putting Aziz's wife on the spot, generalized it as Aziz had done so in Verse: **12; 28.**

Here, it would not be far-fetched to think, that there must be something more to it because ordinarily we do not say it out that the host gave a knife to each invited guest to a banquet. A special mention of her giving a knife to each woman (Verse: **12; 31**) is indeed thought provoking. Hence, another view is that Aziz's wife might have discussed the matter privately with each woman separately assuring her that if she would express her having such an inclination for Yusuf by slashing her hand as a proof of it, she would have things arranged for her too. Having done so, to save everyone's face, she had some fruit served there and gave a knife to each of them in a casual manner as it was customary to set a knife at a formal banquet in those days.

However, when each woman did provide the proof of her having a burning desire for Yusuf by cutting her hand, it had become, manifest that Yusuf's beauty had struck all of them and they all were deeply interested in him. At that Aziz's wife became bold and openly confessed that she indeed had fallen for Yusuf. "There before you is the man about whom you did blame me! I did seduce him and he did firmly save himself guiltless but if now he refuses to obey my order he shall certainly be cast into prison and will be one of those who are disgraced" (Verse; **12:** 32).

Then, the general-consensus of opinion was that it would be Yusuf at fault if he failed to obey his sovereign mistress. After that settled, Aziz's wife laid everything open to Yusuf and gave him the ultimate choice EITHER to go by her command, i.e. avail himself of her liberal offer to him OR else go to prison.

That explains Yusuf praying to Allah, "O my Lord, prison is dearer to me than what *they* invite me to. Unless YOU turn away *their* plot from me I will feel inclined towards *them* and join the ranks of the ignorant" (Verse: **12:** 330).

❖ THE MISSING CUP

(Related to the story)

Then when he (Yusuf) had supplied them with their provisions he placed the drinking-cup in his (full) brother's baggage. Then a crier of the State cried, "O you of the caravan, you are certainly thieves" (Verse: **12:** 70).

"When inquired, "What is it that you are missing"? The crier stated, "We miss the King's drinking-cup and whoever produces it will have the load of a camel and I am responsible for it" (Verses:**12;** 71, 72).

- ❖ One view is that Yusuf had intended to send the cup as a gift to his parents and Allah turned it into what Yusuf ardently desired, i.e. to hold back his full brother, Bin Yamin (Benjamin).
- ❖ Another view is that since it was Allah's plan to have Bin Yamin detained in Egypt, as mentioned in the Holy Qur'an itself, so when the cup was placed in Yusuf's full brother's baggage, the King's drinking-cup also happened to be noticed missing at the time. The proof given in favor of it is that there are two different words "siqarya" stands for Yusuf's drinking-cup (Verse:**12:** 70) and in the Verse **12:** 72 the word, "suwa" for the king's drinking-cup.
- ❖ Still another view is that Yusuf's brothers had played that trick OR used the event in order to get rid of Bin Yamin too as indicated by their saying, "The penalty should be that he, in whose bag the cup is found, should be held, thus we punish the wrongdoers" (Verse:

12: 75). They also said, "if he steals there was a brother of his who did steal before" (Verse; **12:** 77).

Thus, Allah turned the incident around in favor of Bin Yamin because Yusuf could have not detained him under the Egyptian law. Another thing to favor this view is that Yusuf said to his step-brothers, "Do you know what you have done with Yusuf and his brother during your ignorance" (Verse; **12:** 89).

ELEPHANTS AND BIRDS

Prophet Muhammad (peace be upon him) was born 50 days after the following event had taken place:

There was a slave of a Greek merchant, whose name was Abrahah. He was so clever that he succeeded in achieving an influential position in the Abyssinian army occupying Yemen, and later, he himself became the ruler of Yemen. Then, as a king, he devised a dualistic scheme. His obvious mission was to spread out Christianity in Arabia, and his secret motive was to get hold of the trade that was in the hands of the Arabs between the Eastern land and the Byzantine dominions. To accomplish his goals, he built a gorgeous Cathedral in the capital of Yemen. He then arranged a very lavish celebration on the completion of the monumental building. Then, he openly declared, "I shall not rest until I have diverted the Arab's Pilgrimage to this Cathedral".

After that highly provocative public announcement of King Abrahah, it so happened that some unidentified one or two persons entered the Cathedral and shamelessly disgraced it, or maybe set it on fire. It is difficult to rule out here that, all that was not a design on part of Abrahah to make it an excuse to justify his acting out his evil motive. Anyway, he took the stand that, since the devotees of the K'aba had defiled his Cathedral therefore he would not rest until he had destroyed the Khana Kaaba, in Makkah.

So, in A.D. 570 or 571, King Abrahah, set off for Makkah with an army of 60,000 soldiers and about a dozen of elephants. Then, he sent an envoy of his to the chief of Makkah, Abdul Muttalib, with the message that his only aim was to demolish the Kaaba, and if there would be no resistance to that, he had no intention to hurt people of Makkah. To that, Abdul Muttalib stated, "We have no power to fight Abrahah, if Allah wills, Allah will save this House". However, he did agree to personally, meet with King Abrahah.

At the end of their meeting, King Abrahah could not help mentioning to Abdul Muttalib, his own astonishment that Abdul Muttalib had requested him to save his camels but made no mention of not destroying the Kaaba. Regarding that, Abdul Muttalib remarked, "I am the owner of my camels, so I have made a request to you to return them, as for the House, it has its own Owner to defend it". Abrahah said, "I hear that this house is the House of Peace, I have come to destroy its peace". Thereupon, Abdul Muttalib said, "This is Allah's House, Allah has not allowed anyone so far to dominate it". Abrahah said, "We will not return until we have destroyed it". He ordered his troops to advance.

Abdul Muttalib prayed, "O my Lord, protect Your House. Stop them from destroying Your Settlement". After making the prayer, he and his companions went off to the mountains. Then, King Abrahah made preparations to enter Makkah but his special elephant knelt down. All the measures employed to make the elephant go proved to be of no avail. Remarkably enough, it was observed that the elephant would be quickly ready to go in any direction save towards the Kaaba. Every time they attempted to direct the elephant toward Kaaba, the elephant knelt down.

Right then, quite out of blue, there appeared flights of birds of some unfamiliar kind carrying dark red color stones about the size of a pea in their beaks and claws. Upon the soldiers, the birds brought on a heavy shower of the pebbles they were carrying on them and every soldier developed severe itching sores on his skin, and rapidly thereafter, his muscles liquified down to the bone. None of the 60,000 returned home. Some died on the spot, the rest perished on their way back. Within about 3 years of that event, the Abyssinian rule came to end in Yemen.

Some people in Makkah had preserved those stones for a long time. Many poets made that event a subject of their poems. AL-Qur'an: Surah **105** also reminds us of that historical event, albeit, very briefly:

"Have you not seen how your Lord dealt with the companions of the elephant? Did Allah not cause their plan to end in vain and send down on them swarms of birds that pelted them with stones of baked clay? Then, Allah rendered them like straw eaten up by cattle."

MILKY WAY

Allah, in paradise, under which the streams flow, catechized Adam and Eve, and as such, the human being was competently prepared to survive and enjoy the sojourn in this world, and to lead life in the prescribed manner in order to trace the way back to the paradise.

Islam requires of us to set an example for others of how to lead life.

Islam requires of us to seek common points in other disciplines to avoid disputes, to respect (not merely to tolerate) other faiths, and to treat everyone in a just manner. Disliking a person's bad habit or bad behavior is one thing, disliking that person is another. The former is appropriate, the latter is not acceptable.

Violence is not the way of Islam; partly-quoted or misinterpreted Quranic Verses are either related to war or hypocrites (some seemingly contradictions, gender issues, e.g. polygamy etc., I have discussed in my book, "Islam and Obstacles to It).

Islam excites us to make scientific progress and to remain submissive to God.

Islam instructs us to avoid rumors, quarrels, suspicion and spying in social life. Islam teaches us to be objective, not to exploit and safeguard against being exploited.

Islam has given to men and women their just rights and equal dignity as human beings.

The Holy Qur'an says that revelation carries its own proofs and rejecters miss their own chance. Not wealth but righteousness attains the happy end. Allah is the only Reality. No soul should despair because of its sin. Allah's Mercy is unbounded; repent before judgment comes.

We become certain of something if we see it or if we become sure of it through our sound judgment and logical reasoning. If we do come to believe in God then the Day of Judgment becomes an unquestionable Reality because God has spoken of it. Our eyes can deceive us, our judgment can be wrong, but God is infallible. Not infrequently, we do observe dishonesty and injustice flourishing in this world. This leads some to believe that there is no God, while some use this very observation as proof for the coming of the Day of Judgment. Evil and mischief may spread, but Allah will restore the balance in the End. Allah created Purity, Harmony and Law, evil is doomed to perish.

We simply cannot afford to stand or get lost in this world's fashionable fair. Fortunately, we have the "Map" that leads us to paradise - our real home. Our Real Home promised to us by Allah, but not unconditionally.

FACTOR FAITH

❖ During my High School days, once I saw the following headline in a newspaper: "Geographers, Attention, Attention". What it said was, "It is a common observation that if any airplane high up in the air keeps on circling around any given point on the earth, it stays around the same point. In other words if an airplane would go straight up a few miles and then come back straight down, it would land on the same spot on the ground it had taken off. All this proves that the earth is stationary, otherwise, that given point within a second would have gone somewhere far away because that airplane had no connection with the earth at the time. To dispel this confusion, one has to understand the range of the centrifugal force of the revolving earth. Needless to say, more knowledge may be needed to stay on a truth confidently.

❖ Once, right opposite to Mayo hospital, adjacent to King Edward Medical College, a medicine-man was selling some snakebite remedy. He was proclaiming, "Doctors have only one remedy and that is - Cut Off, ask these fools that if a snake happens to bite on someone's head, will you cut that person's head off"? It is notable that he particularly emphasized, that anyone lacking faith in his product should not buy it. However, the overall impact was, that people started buying the snakebite remedy from him like hot cakes.

❖ Sometimes, I look for a thing and do not find it but after searching for it at other places when I go back to the same place again with a firm conviction that it has to or must be there, Lo Behold, I find it. Why my first search so often fails is a question that should be easy to answer.

"SEEK AND YE SHALL FIND"
ALTA PETE
(Aim for the Highest)

ABOUT THE AUTHOR

Ahmed K. Nazir, M.D. was born in Rawalpindi, Pakistan. There, he graduated from Gordon College, then joined King Edward Medical College, Lahore, Pakistan as a medical student. In his early medical career, Dr. Nazir served as a physician in Pakistan and England. Before joining psychiatry residency, he obtained some postgraduate training in other basic specialities of the field of Medicine. Dr Nazir has practiced psychiatry in America for 25 years including a term in US Air Force as a psychiatrist. Some newspapers and magazines have published several of his articles in English and Urdu. Dr. Nazir likes checkers, music, poetry, attentive reading, and studying the Holy Qur'an.

OTHER BOOKS BY THE SAME AUTHOR

Is God Man-made

In Light of Al-Qur'an - learning how to live

Dispositions

Balanced Personality

Attitudes

Desires and Values

Basic Human Nature - good, bad, both, neither

Islam and Obstacles to It

Sham'ayel (in Urdu)